How to Get and Give Love

— Relationship Maps

5 minute maps to 3 easy steps

Benna Sherman (signature)

By Benna Z Sherman, Ph.D.
Licensed Psychologist

How to Get and Give Love
— *Relationship Maps*

ISBN: 147015403X

Benna Z. Sherman, Ph.D.

Licensed Psychologist

Suite 304B

479 Jumpers Hole Road

Severna Park, Maryland 21146

(410) 544-9564

email: DrBenna@DrBennaSherman.com

website: DrBennaSherman.com

blog: blog.bennasherman.com

Facebook: Facebook.com/DrBennaSherman

Twitter: twitter.com/DrBenna

♥

*Dedicated to my most important relationships,
the loves of my life—
my husband and my children*

♥

Table of Contents

♥

It's the only map I have.
I figured it was better than nothing.

♥

A parable

*T*wo tourists are thoroughly lost in The City. Tourist One pulls out a map and, pointing, says, "We should go this way."

They proceed for a while in this fashion, with Tourist One consulting the map regularly and directing them.

Having arrived at a seedy-looking part of town, Tourist Two turns to Tourist One and says, "Are you sure this is the way?"

Tourist One, feeling defensive and not at all sure, says, "I'm just following the map! Look at the map for yourself!"

Tourist Two looks at the map and notices that it is in fact a map not of The City but of Someplace Else.

"You fool!" Tourist Two says to Tourist One. "This isn't even a map of The City!"

Tourist One shrugs and replies, "But it's the only map I have. I figured it was better than nothing."

Acknowledgment

*M*uch of the material for this book was first introduced in columns written over several years for <u>The Medical News</u>, <u>Your Health Magazine</u>, and <u>The Capital</u>, all of which have graciously waived all rights to the material.

Many of the scenarios described in these chapters are composites of situations faced by couples whom I've seen in psychotherapy in my private practice. No particular individuals are intended to be accurately represented. All individuals and couples are, however, gratefully acknowledged for their contributions to the therapeutic process. It's the loving and generous commitment that people demonstrate to their partners, sometimes in disguised ways, that has provided the guidance for this book.

♥

We all end up with a map collection. Some of those maps will turn out to be helpful as we navigate through the rest of our lives. Some of them will turn out to limit us more than they can assist us.

♥

Introduction

*T*here are all kinds of maps. Mostly we think of lines and squiggles on paper showing things like streets, rivers, and legal boundaries. We use these maps to help us get around safely and efficiently, assisting us to move predictably from one place to another. These maps represent the geography of the physical world and they're immensely helpful for moving around in that world. One of the first things people do when they move or travel to a new place is buy (or download) a map.

What about guidelines for moving through the geography of our interpersonal world? Where do we go for a map that will help us navigate through relationships? Human beings aren't generally solitary creatures by choice. It's the wish of most people to be involved successfully with at least one other person in an emotionally intimate way. Many people find, however, that crossing 3,000 miles of physical space is a snap compared to navigating the emotional space between people. It would be helpful if emotional territory also had maps to assist us in moving around safely and efficiently. Such a map could indicate where any given path might lead and help us to make informed choices about directions to follow (or avoid) to end up in a particular place.

From the time we're born, we're involved (successfully or not) in relationships of one sort or another. We begin generally with parents, expand our explorations to include other family members, and gradually add relationships with people outside the family – baby-sitters, doctors, teachers, neighbors. Each encounter adds to our personal collection of information about how people get from one place to another with each other and helps us to construct general outline maps of various kinds of relationships.

We all end up with a map collection. Some of those maps will turn out to be helpful as we navigate through the rest of our lives. Some of them will turn out to limit us more than they can assist us.

It can be hard to resist using our maps without regard to their appropriateness. People will sometimes cling fiercely to an old map just because it's their favorite or the only one they have, even when they know (or suspect) that it's inappropriate. Sometimes those maps will contain useful information. But sometimes they give you a false sense of knowing where you're going when they can really only lead you astray. The most important rule for map users is to remember that you need to construct a map of Here and Now.

For example, imagine that you grew up in a large, chaotic household where you only got enough to eat if you grabbed food faster than others. That map may have helped you survive as a child, but it may not serve you well years later when your host at an elegant dinner party is a prospective employer. In fact, using that map may guarantee that you don't get where you were hoping to be.

Be prepared for the necessity of updating your maps or even throwing away old maps and making new ones. Collect data that's specific to Here and Now, data that reflects the people you're with now. Be prepared for getting lost in unpleasant territory if you use a map that is not up-to-date or is inappropriate.

In **How to Get and Give Love – Relationship Maps,** you'll learn to recognize when old maps are keeping you at a frustrating distance from your partner. You'll learn how to construct new maps that will bring you closer. You'll learn skills and strategies for navigating the territory between you while also increasing the likelihood that you'll get your own personal needs met. With your new maps, whatever terrain you may face, you'll know how to travel from where you are to where you want to be. And you'll do it while feeling loved and being loving.

Each chapter is an essay that can stand independently. Taken together, they construct a course in building and maintaining a healthy and satisfying relationship with your partner. The chapters are intended to be used one at a time, to be read, thought about, and shared. Take the time to field test the strategies with the people in your life. Think of these field trips as opportunities to collect data that will allow you to construct helpful, accurate maps. Then, enjoy the trip!

♥

Listening
Understanding
Responding

♥

Without these, nothing else will be quite enough.
With them, anything is possible.

♥

It's as easy as
1-2-3

*C*reating and sustaining a successful relationship with your partner rests on three fundamental principles. Without these, nothing else will be quite enough. With them, anything is possible.

1. **LISTENING**

Listening means paying active attention when your partner
speaks. There are many ways to demonstrate active listening. Eye
contact is one of the most important. When you maintain eye contact you indicate that your focus is on your partner. Eye contact
says, more than words ever could, that you're openly and directly
attending to your partner. It also conveys a willingness to participate in the communication process. Failure to maintain eye contact suggests either an unwillingness to participate or an inability
to participate openly and honestly.

Turning your body, particularly your chest (and heart), toward
your partner communicates your commitment to connection.
There's an implied message of orienting not just your body but
also your thoughts and feelings toward your partner. You communicate some more through body language about how you're
listening by the way you hold your arms and legs. Are your arms
crossed over your chest or your legs crossed at the knee? These
postures suggest that you are protecting yourself or keeping yourself closed. Active listening involves openness to what's being
presented.

Maintaining your attention exclusively on your partner when he or she is speaking – no TV or newspaper, for example, competing for your attention – demonstrates that you consider your partner's words a priority. Whatever your words might say (like, "Yes, yes, I'm paying attention."), in the end it's your behavior that'll be believed. If your behavior shows attention to the papers on your desk or the TV across the room, your partner feels that your priorities are, at best, mixed. When you clearly put aside other distractions, you communicate that you value your partner's words, thoughts, and feelings.

One of the most powerful experiences that we can have is to feel that someone has truly listened to us. It's amazingly heady, like being on stage before an attentive audience. It communicates that someone has judged you to be worthy of their time and energy, that someone values what you might have to say, that someone cares about what you might be feeling. To be listened to is to be elevated. When it's someone whom you love who's truly listening to you it's to feel beloved in return. It's to feel, however briefly, that you're the center of the universe.

When you're the one doing the listening you're in a very powerful position, for you have the power to give this feeling to someone. It's the power to lift someone above the daily routine. It's the power to respond to the craving that we all have to be attended to by someone. When you can give such a gift to someone whom you love it's especially gratifying.

2. Understanding

A critical piece of any communication process is understanding. No communication can be considered successful if the listener hasn't understood the speaker. No speaker can be confident that successful communication has occurred if there isn't evidence of understanding by the listener.

The speaker feels that someone is truly interested in the content of the communication when a listener demonstrates a desire to understand. Listeners can demonstrate a desire to understand by asking questions, requesting clarification, or soliciting details. Comments like, "This happened yesterday?", or, "Your fever was how high?", or, "By 'upset', do you mean scared or angry?" are evidence that, not only are you listening, but you have a desire to understand what it is that you're being told. Questions, clarifications, and solicitations convey that you share the speaker's belief that this content is important. To share even such a simple belief is to align yourself with someone, at least briefly. It's as if to say, "This matters to you, so it matters to me too. Let me move over to share space with you and see things from your perspective."

At the same time that there's evidence of someone's wish to understand, it's reassuring to get signals that you are being understood. There can be gestures, like a head-nod. Or there might be comments, like, "Oh, my", or "How wonderful!" These are signals to the speaker that the listener is receiving the content and relating to it. This lets the speaker know that communication has successfully occurred.

A powerful indicator of a listener's understanding is the ability to paraphrase back what was said. If you can, in your own words, give back to me the message that I intended to give to you, then I can rest comfortably in the knowledge that you understood my meaning. Perhaps what you paraphrase to me doesn't match my intended message. Then I have the opportunity to present my message again, but differently, in an effort to have it received in a way that more closely matches my intentions.

When two individuals participate in communication, there's always the possibility that there will be a difference between transmission and reception. Transmission is what the speaker is sending; reception is what the listener is receiving. They're not always the same thing. Just as in the children's games of Whisper Down the Alley, Telephone, or Telegraph, the messages can get grotesquely garbled between people. There might even be agreement about the words involved, but the interpretations of those words might be very different. If understanding is the goal, it's critical to confirm that the intended transmission matches the actual reception.

When transmission and reception don't match, there's a feeling for both participants of frustration and of being separated by a gulf of space not shared. But to be understood is to feel a sense of communion, a feeling of being joined to someone by a moment of shared perspective.

③. <u>Responding</u>

Responding means simply that you do something because you listened to and understood someone's message. Your behavior has been influenced by what you heard and understood. Clearly, then, one potential value to response is that it can confirm that you listened, you understood, and you chose to behave in some way that reflected your understanding of your partner's messages. Your response may or may not always be the one that your partner was hoping to get. But if it demonstrates listening and understanding, it goes a long way toward persuading your partner that you're trying.

Responding isn't the same thing as obeying. It is of course possible that responding to someone's message may mean complying with a request. You may respond by doing something that your partner asks of you, like being the one to put the kids to bed tonight or being the one to cook dinner. But it doesn't have to mean doing what you've been asked to do. If someone asks you to do something that's beyond your means or beyond your comfort level, you may be unable or unwilling to comply. Yet you may nonetheless do something to try to be responsive to the message that you received. Your response would make clear that you listened and understood. For example, perhaps your partner asked you to move in together. You didn't feel ready for that, but you did want to respond to the message you received concerning sharing time and space. So responding might involve giving your partner a key to your apartment.

In the same way, if someone shares with you their grief over a loss, it isn't that they expect you to bring back who or what they've lost. What they're hoping for is responsiveness – evidence that you have, through listening and understanding, made a connection with their pain, and that you wish to do something for them (like sharing sympathetic words or a hug).

People want to feel that they matter. When people interact, it's universal to hope that we have some kind of impact on each other. When you're responsive to someone– when your behavior is affected by their words or feelings– you give them evidence of that impact. When you're responsive to someone who loves you, your responsiveness is all the more valuable, because you're so valuable to them. Responsiveness says in the most telling way, "I care enough about you to invest energy and effort in listening and understanding and doing something about the messages that I heard and understood."

When your behavior indicates that you have truly listened to your partner's messages, understood them, and wish to be responsive, it's a very loving experience for your partner. It's in fact the experience people are most fundamentally seeking within relationships.

More important than the outcome is the process. The specific response is less important than the feeling that the process has been genuine and loving and has led, therefore, to some kind of demonstration of caring. When the process is successful in this way, the relationship itself feels successful. Without it, all the bells and whistles in the world won't make the relationship feel right.

It's as easy as 1-2-3

Everything that follows in the subsequent chapters is founded on these three principles of relationship behavior. The book is divided into three sections matching these three principles. You will find however that the assignment of any given essay to a particular section is at best a rough match. The principles interweave throughout many of the articles and assignment was simply an attempt to make the best fit. As you make your way through the following essays, consider occasionally revisiting this chapter. With these three principles firmly established and nurtured in your relationship, everything is possible.

♥

Listening
Without it there is no relationship.

♥

Listening

*L*istening is an immensely powerful tool. It's critical from the very beginning of our lives as social creatures. When babies cry or gurgle or coo they need to feel that their caretakers are listening. They need to see those eyes looking back. They need to see the caretaker's head swivel in their direction when they make noises. It's these responses that make them feel important and safe. They need to feel that at that moment they are the center of someone's universe.

When those babies grow up, they still need to feel listened to. And being listened to still communicates that they are important. And it still feels like safety and warmth and love.

It is impossible to overstate the value of listening. All successful interpersonal connection depends on it. There is no stage of life, for an individual or for a relationship, in which listening is not a critical component. When it is done well the message of validation and the experience of communion are profound.

It is the first step of three (Listening, Understanding, and Responding) in initiating, developing, and maintaining relationships. Without it, there can be no relationship.

What follows in this section are principles and vignettes demonstrating why listening matters, how it affects people, and what to do to improve its functioning in your dealings with other people.

♥

There's little that you can say that will ever
have the power of how well you listen.

♥

How to make someone fall in love with you

Mindy was describing her latest love. I was curious about what had so powerfully attracted her to a man she described as "average" in most ways.

"When I'm with him, he makes me feel that I'm the only other person in the room. He makes me feel that I'm the most interesting person he's ever met, as if everything I say is fascinating. His eyes are glued to mine. The way he pays attention to my every word makes me feel beautiful."

Mistresses, gigolos, and romance novelists have known the secret for a long time. The secret to winning a campaign for someone's heart doesn't really reside in hair, makeup, clothes, a great body, or even witty conversation. More powerful in drawing someone to you than the Porsche, the gourmet cooking, or the respected profession Is ... listening.

Mickey was trying to explain to me why he'd been carrying on an affair for several months with a woman from work. He loved his wife, Laura, but he felt a kind of loneliness within his marriage. He described his wife as more beautiful than the woman from work, smarter, and more talented. He confessed that, frankly, the sex was better with his wife. Why then an affair? He sighed and the lines in his face softened as he answered, "She listens to me."

He went on to say, "She's interested in every detail of my day. She's even interested in the technical details of my job. Laura is always bored by anything to do with work."

I asked Mickey which he'd prefer – the affair or his marriage to Laura, but with Laura listening to him the way that the other woman was listening to him. He had no difficulty at all in choosing.

"Laura's the woman I've always wanted. If she were listening, then I'd know she cared about me. And I'd have everything I needed."

What is it about listening that has this magical effect on people? Think for a moment what it means to you when someone listens to you. When someone listens to you, you feel important. When someone listens to you, that person is in effect choosing you from among all the many things to which he or she could pay attention. It makes you feel attractive. When someone listens to you, he or she implies an interest in what you have to say, what you think, what you care about. It makes you feel very connected. To be listened to feels elevating. It's a tremendously positive experience.

Psychology research has found that feelings are often reciprocal – we tend to like the people that we believe like us. If someone listens to you, then you tend to believe that that person likes you. It follows that you'll like them back. If that person listens so attentively that you feel loved, then you tend to feel love toward that person in return.

The same thing happens in reverse. If you feel that someone doesn't like you, then you tend not to like him. If someone doesn't listen to you, you may feel unloved and unimportant in that person's life. In that case the reciprocal feeling is to demote that person in your life.

If you want to attract someone to you, help that person see that you feel attracted to her. The easiest way I know to make a person feel attractive is through listening. The message, "You're attractive, you're special," is communicated. The most successful escort or companion is always the one who listens. Whatever else this companion does or doesn't do, it's the listening that will be valued most highly.

In an issue of <u>People</u> magazine, a very attractive actress was explaining why a particular not-very-hunky actor was the break-out sex symbol of the cast. She explained that his character was a sensitive guy who listens. "Listening is sexy."

We often talk about the silver-tongued speaker. But the real power lies with the good listener. There's little that you can say that will ever have the power of how well you listen.

♥

The more he wanted to know about her, the more
interested she was in learning about him.

♥

Getting to know you,
getting to know all about you

*F*rom the time that we are born, we crave the experience of feeling that we are truly known and understood. We long for those moments in which we feel that someone really wants to know who we are. Infants want to look up into their parents' eyes and see those eyes looking back. Little kids come home from pre-school and want to have Mommy or Daddy listen to every detail of their day AND show interest. The wanting to be listened to, wanting to be known by another person, doesn't stop when you grow up. One of the most compelling events between two people occurs when they come together in a communion of sharing in which they both feel listened to and understood.

Jennifer was hoping, without much optimism, that this party would be different. She generally had a reasonably good time – she was personable, not particularly shy, had a decent knack with small talk. It was easy enough to talk to people and she was attractive enough to get her share of male attention. What she was hoping for was more than that. She was hoping that this evening would produce one of those rare events where she met someone whom she wished to know better and who seemed to care about knowing her.

The first half hour passed pleasantly but without much substance. Then she found herself in a conversation with Bob. It had started out like a thousand other conversations – he asked what she did (she was a legislative aide to a Congresswoman) and where she lived (Bethesda) and a few other run of the mill questions. She noticed though that he was really paying attention to the answers and that he'd ask follow-up questions. His attention never wavered from her, even as the party swirled around them.

Then he started to ask her probing questions about how she <u>felt</u> about her work. It was wonderful to have someone demonstrate this much interest in her and in her life. The more he wanted to know about her, the more interested she was in learning about him. It was very heady to feel that he was more interested in learning about her than in telling her about himself.

When she did ask questions about him, he seemed very pleased with her authentic interest. He shared that when she talked about her feelings about her work that it brought up some significant questions for him about his own work. It was so exciting to him to realize that she was completely interested in hearing his thoughts and feelings.

They spent the rest of the evening talking. When the party broke up, they transferred their conversation to a late night diner and talked for another couple of hours. Sometimes he was talking and she was listening. Sometimes she was talking and he was listening. They seemed to find everything about each other fascinating. They covered everything – politics (he was a Republican, she a Democrat), movies (they both loved Monty Python), travel (they were both eager to do it), books (they agreed that J.K. Rowling should be knighted), religion (he was observant and she was questioning), and roommate horror stories (of which they both had horrific and hysterical examples). It was surprising to discover that they didn't need to agree on everything to feel good about it. It was more important to share their thoughts and feel that the other person was interested. They each felt a kind of validation at being listened to so attentively. The event clearly transcended the issues, and whether they held identical opinions was irrelevant.

The next day, at the gym, Jennifer told her best friend, Heidi, about Bob and about her evening. She described how they'd talked practically all night and how she felt that she knew him so well already. What got Heidi's attention wasn't how well Jennifer felt that she knew Bob. It was how Jennifer described feeling so well understood <u>by</u> Bob. Heidi could see it coming – this was going to be another bridesmaid's dress to add to her collection. She crossed her fingers that the words "lavender" and "ruffles" did not come up in the same sentence…

♥

Listen more and explain less.

♥

As any fool can plainly see

*A*ll human beings tend to believe that what appears to them to be The Truth is in fact the truth. Women, however, tend to be particularly invested in their partners seeing the truth the same way they do, sometimes to the exclusion of listening to an alternative point of view.

Walking in after the Den meeting, Mona sent Lenny upstairs to do his homework and sat down on the couch next to Roger.

"Rog, we have to talk about Scouts. Lenny says he wants to quit."

"Fine by me."

"Rog, this is the third thing in a row that he's started and wanted to quit within the first couple of months."

"He told me he thinks it's boring. He'd rather build his models and just hang out with Jason."

"Well, sometimes things are boring, at least for awhile. Does that mean that he can quit things so quickly? Shouldn't we be teaching him a lesson about commitment?"

"Mona, he's 8. Maybe he should be learning not to waste his time when he doesn't have to with stuff that bores him."

"I think this is important. He should at least stay 'til Christmas."

"Fine. You think this is way more important than I do. Do what you think is best."

[Some might see this as a victory for Mona and expect her to stop the discussion here. Having the authority to decide unilaterally for her son is not what Mona wants in this case. She wants Roger to see the situation the same way that she does. Furthermore, she believes that once he <u>properly</u> understands the situation, he will inevitably see that the only proper course of action is the one that she believes in.]

"Rog, I think that he should stay the course and learn that if he's patient, things get more interesting."

"Mona, I said 'okay'; do what you want about Scouts. Why do I also have to agree with you?"

[Mona does not want him just to go along with her, whether it's to humor her, get her off his back, be easygoing, or even just trust her parenting judgment. She wants him to think this the way that she thinks it. If he does that, then she's confident that he'll see her answer is the answer, the answer that any fool can plainly see. If he doesn't, then she has to worry about his intelligence and judgment. But she also worries about their alignment and connection. If they're not on the same page about this, are they well-matched as people? A misalignment feels worrisome.]

This is an interesting stuck place for many couples. She is hopeful that his position is in error as a result of simply not understanding the situation completely. Therefore, she will continue to discuss it, and, worse, explain it, until he is sufficiently clear on things that his position "spontaneously" shifts to mirror hers.

Some men get very angry at this juncture, feeling that their perfectly legitimate take on things is not only being rejected but treated as stupid. Some men realize that they're in a no-win situation. Since they really don't see things the same way, they can either be wrong with a divergent position or they can be wrong by giving in. Alternately, they can be dishonest either with their partner or with themselves and claim that they now agree. Some men get highly practiced at getting out of this spot by taking time to "think things over" and then coming back with a "spontaneous conversion".

Women, for their part, will often deny honestly and vigorously that they're looking for someone to parrot their opinions. They truly want someone with an independent mind. The problem is that they also expect that that independent mind will independently come to a conclusion that is the same as theirs. A divergent opinion is indication of a failure of the thinking process, and possibly a failure of their connection. So, trusting that their partners are intelligent and honorable, they proceed to offer endless assistance with the thinking process in the indefatigable commitment to helping their partners get it right.

Ultimately, women need to give more consideration to the possibility that a man's perspective, when divergent from hers, could still be valid. It's disrespectful and downright unfair to attempt relentlessly to change your partner's thinking simply because it doesn't reflect your own. Consider that if he wasn't a fool when you married him, maybe he hasn't become one. Listen more and explain less.

Consider that a divergent point of view may be something that this relationship can absorb without damage and without any weakening of the connection between partners. The risk is in <u>less</u> listening, not more.

♥

The <u>business</u> of being a family crowds out
the <u>reason</u> for being a family.

♥

May I have your attention, please

*M*ost of us are lucky enough to have very full lives. We work, we have a choice of options for play, we have family (children and/or parents) to take care of, and we have community responsibilities and opportunities. We have a lot of demands on our attention. It's particularly true for those of us with kids in the house who need or want our attention a lot. It's easy to spend all of your available attention on those things that jump up and down and demand it. But what of the attentional needs of our partners and our relationships?

Sometimes we have the illusion that we're paying attention to our partners and relationships because we've spoken to each other. How often though is this exchange of words more likely to be about the <u>business</u> of a family and household rather than a true interpersonal sharing?

Think about it – what opportunity for communion is there in communication that only addresses issues like who's picking up the dry-cleaning or which week is better for the trip to the beach? Of course these things need to be discussed. The problem is that this communion-free communication can become the only communication between partners. It can even obscure the fact that you've become co-managers of a household instead of intimate partners.

Most of us start households and families because we're engaged in intimate relationships. Somehow, insidiously, the <u>business</u> of being a family crowds out the <u>reason</u> for being a family.

But we need the communion of relationships. That's what builds the bonds between people. Those bonds provide the strength and resiliency to carry us through challenges, demands, and hardships. These challenges and such can be of many different kinds – a family's relocation to new schools and new jobs, a parent's or a child's illness, a parent's job loss, a child's special needs, etc. Our ability to cope depends heavily on our sense that we are part of a relationship that is nurturing and sustaining. People who experience these kinds of events in the absence of such relationships have a much harder time and often experience much more stress and illness. Communion protects us from the worst impacts of stress. People who do not have intimate family relationships to sustain them are sometimes fortunate enough to be supported by the communion of community.

In order to establish these bonds, we need to pay adequate attention to the significant people in our lives, and to do so in meaningful personal ways. It is unlikely that this will be accomplished casually. We can't depend on it happening as a natural outgrowth of family life. Families are too busy and have too many demands/opportunities that keep them apart. Partners need to make specific, intentional plans to come together in activities that allow them to pay meaningful attention to each other.

These times of communion can be formal – like a romantic candlelit dinner in a fine restaurant. They can be informal – iced tea shared on the deck as the sun is going down. But what they must have in common is that there are no significant distractions vying for attention. When attention is focused, the moment has the magic to allow communion to occur. Your partner can feel that he or she is your priority if your attention is focused only on him or her. Your partner needs to experience this sense of being special and important to you.

The next element is repetition. These moments when attention is not diverted must be repeated regularly. Bonds are built and strengthened when communion occurs regularly. You wouldn't try to nourish your body by eating only occasionally, when the opportunity just happens to present itself. Relationships require regular, frequent nourishment also.

Partners need to make a commitment to come together regularly and frequently and share their attention only with each other. The moments can be big or small, but they're magic either way.

♥

Putting aside your own wishes to pay
attention to your partner's wishes

♥

Give 'em what they want

*H*ow well do you know your partner? How well do you know what he or she likes, enjoys, is scared by, thrilled by, warmed by? Are you a successful gift-giver? Your gift-giving success is directly linked to how well you know your partner. Critical to knowing your partner is having listened to him or her over time. Listening means, among other components, that you have put aside your own egocentric view of the world and made space to attend to your partner's view of the world. Successful listening can't take place unless you can, sometimes, put aside thinking about your own experience. If, when you're supposedly listening, you're thinking about how *you* feel, then you can't be absorbing as effectively whatever it is that your partner is sharing with you.

If the interaction with your partner is compromised by fractured attention – some to your partner's words, some to your own thoughts about yourself – you're less likely to walk away with an accurate, deep, or broad understanding of your partner. You'll have a harder time knowing what it is that your partner needs and wants. The way to secure an adequate knowledge base about your partner is to listen, to pay attention, even when your partner's interests diverge from your own.

Their fifth anniversary was a month away, and they were both working hard to make a very special occasion. In service of surprise, neither had revealed to the other even a hint about plans.

As the time got closer, they each had to clarify a few critical details, so oblique questions started coming, in supposedly casual ways. He asked her what size shirt she wore; she asked him if his hiking boots were in good shape. As the date approached, he got a feverish look in his eyes; she got a kind of dreamy glazed look. He'd jump up from his laptop and yell, "Score!" and then sit down and try to look casual. Other times, she'd say, "Oh, that is so romantic!", and look up from her magazine and smile at him in a particularly loving way.

Their anniversary was January 25th. That evening they met at their favorite Italian restaurant. The table was set with candles and their favorite wine was on the table. They toasted their anniversary and kissed across the table. They were both so excited to reveal their surprise presents to each other.

He said, "Let me go first, pretty please? You are going to go wild over this and I cannot wait one more minute to see the look on your face!" He pulled an envelope from his jacket pocket and slid it across the table. Her imagination started racing as she saw that there were airline tickets enclosed.

"We're going to …?"

"That's right! The Super Bowl! Can you believe it?! I couldn't believe that I could get the tickets. Of course, it cost a small fortune on e-Bay, but this is a special occasion, and I was sparing no expense to make you the most amazing fifth anniversary in history!" He was positively beaming.

"So, what did you get me?" He was grinning from ear to ear, confident that she couldn't match the excitement of his gift to her but knowing that it was something totally cool, because she'd been grinning like a Cheshire Cat for weeks.

She slid an envelope over to him. His grin slipped a little as he slipped out the brochures for the bed-and-breakfast. There were photographs of couples walking hand in hand on the beach, hiking the "gentle" trails, and joining all the other guests at high tea.

She smiled lovingly at him. "Isn't it the most romantic thing you've ever seen? The Guide gave it a "3Heart" rating for anniversaries."

As his eyes continued to roam over the brochures, they alighted on the date of their reservations. The last time he was this devastated his older brother had told him there was no Santa Claus. He was speechless.

Fortunately, at that moment their waiter arrived with their appetizers; and they each had some time to formulate a response to their mutual dilemmas.

She went first.

"The game sounds great, of course, but you would really prefer the Super Bowl to the bed-and-breakfast?" she asked gently but incredulously.

He said, "The bed-and-breakfast looks very romantic, but, gee, the Super Bowl is, well, the Super Bowl. I thought you'd be really excited about it. It only happens once a year, and my team's in it. "

"<u>Your</u> team's in the Super Bowl, so you thought that <u>I'd</u> want to go to it? When have I ever enjoyed large crowds of people all screaming at the tops of their lungs? I've told you that I hate those kinds of events."

Their surprise and disappointment at not getting the reactions that they'd expected was matched, however, by the sincerity of their intentions. As the dinner and the conversation continued, what they both got to express was how much they'd wanted to make the perfect anniversary for their partner. They toasted their love and, by the time the dessert tray was brought, they were able to laugh about the muck up. She looked at him lovingly and grinned.

"Well, at least I know what to get you for your next birthday. Next time I'll get you what <u>you</u> want instead of what <u>I</u> want."

He smiled back. "Yeah, you know, this reminds me of when I was nine and I got my mom a baseball glove for her birthday. It was a great gift, but for me, not for her."

As her anniversary gift to him, he took his best friend to the Super Bowl. As his gift to her, they changed the bed-and-breakfast reservations to her birthday. And he exchanged the jersey that he'd bought her for a dozen long-stemmed red roses.

When they really listened to each other, when they put aside their own wishes in service of listening to their partner's wishes, they got it. Love + Listening is a pretty powerful equation.

♥

<u>Being</u> with your partner is more important
than what you're <u>doing</u>.

♥

Coming together and growing apart

*W*hen couples are courting, partners often say things like, "Oh, I don't care what we do, as long as we do it together." This is often said with a dreamy smile and followed by a kiss. During this period of early bliss, it's easy to sit through operas that you hate, films in languages that you don't speak, sports events for sports you couldn't care less about, painting walls that are not yours, and so on. It is eminently clear that the important part is being together. The content of the events during which you are together matters relatively little. It seems sometimes that there just aren't enough hours in the day to see enough of your beloved.

If you are lucky enough to marry your beloved, the early part of the marriage is often a continuation of this phase, where togetherness is the guiding force for choosing how to spend your time. In fact, you would choose to spend your time in an undesirable activity shared with your partner in preference to a desirable activity without your partner. It's all very romantic. It also serves to strengthen the bonds that are forming between you and your partner. You are creating connectedness and developing a shared history, as well as affirming that the fact of <u>being</u> with your partner is more important than the nature of what you're <u>doing</u>.

Then life happens. You generally get to see your partner every day. It doesn't take any special intention to spend time with your partner – he or she is at your dinner table every evening, in your bed every night, and sitting across from you during your morning coffee. Now other things are asserting themselves in your life – friends you haven't been spending much time with, hobbies you've been neglecting, extended family that wants more of your attention, work that could use some extra investment of your time and energy, self-care like exercise or meditation or church attendance.

Choosing how to spend your time is no longer a decision that is dominated by wanting to be with your partner for more precious-but-rare time. Because it's less rare, it isn't as obviously precious. Now other factors are figured in too. Gradually, the question of the nature of the activity takes on more importance in the decision. Now the inherent value or interest or fun of the activity itself weighs significantly in the decision-making process.

Naturally, no matter how close or similar you and your partner may be, you do not have identical interests and commitments. Since together time is no longer rare, it seems reasonable to start spending more apart time, time where each of you can pursue your individual interests and tend to individual demands and needs. It's not only natural; it's necessary. Even in a relationship, individuals must be preserved and nurtured.

The danger lies in the potential for an insidious, gradual divergence of the paths of the two partners. At some point, the decision of whether to attend a particular event may be completely uninfluenced by the opportunity to be together or the importance of spending time together. At this point, the decision about whether to attend may be influenced exclusively by whether the event is fun, or interesting, or important to you personally. Partners often have been developing different interests unencumbered by their partners and their partner's interests, resulting in partners spending less and less time together. We now have two people developing separate paths, separate histories. Time spent together now is in fact rare but is no longer considered precious. It often feels instead burdensome and an inconvenience. In fact, you have less and less in common with your partner and are spending little or no time trying to develop or sustain common interests.

At some point, it may start to seem obvious that you and your partner have few if any interests in common. The bonds that you were strengthening with shared activities in the early phases of your relationship have been getting frayed by a lack of those same activities. As you each pursued your individual interests, you developed as individuals but not as partners.

But individual development doesn't have to come at the cost of your relationship. It takes a sustained and conscious intention to nurture the shared relationship path. It takes repeatedly (but not always) putting aside individual interest in service of the relationship's needs. It means going to those operas, sports events, etc. in which you have no individual interest simply because it's important and valuable to be with your partner.

Choose to walk a path with your partner, not for the scenery but for the company.

♥

By listening so well, you will be listened to as well.

♥

Pacing

*T*here is a concept in therapy called, "pacing". It is a technique for joining someone and creating rapport. Essentially, it means figuring out where someone is, emotionally, and meeting him there. This is a way of establishing a connection that is experienced by the recipient as positive, accepting, and validating.

The first step in pacing involves directing highly focused attention to someone. This is attention without distractions, without any competition for your thoughts. This must happen first if you are going to perceive and understand accurately where someone is. Then you must put aside your own separate orientation and make the effort to assume that of the other person. It is when you commit to this temporary selflessness that you can most effectively join with another person. For the listener, this means putting aside, for a time, any sense of your own agenda and proceeding with a commitment to know and understand the agenda of the other person. This is true listening, not just waiting your turn to speak, not preparing your response, not defending your position. Your only intention here is to know what the other person is thinking, feeling, and needing.

The listener figures this out not only by actively listening to the words being spoken, and the tone in which they're spoken, but also by attending to the other person's body language. This fully committed and comprehensive attentiveness pays off by producing a deep and undistorted awareness of the other person.

The goal is to pay such close attention, with such a commitment to putting self aside, that you can join the other person in their space, whatever it may happen to be at that moment.

When you accomplish this kind of joining, the other person experiences a sense of connection and validation that is very elevating and quite powerful. Particularly in an intimate relationship, this also brings feelings of closeness and trust.

Once this pacing and joining has been achieved, then the person who is experiencing this powerful connection also becomes uniquely open to *receiving* input from the person on the other end of the connection. This rapport creates both trust and receptiveness.

In effect, because you have so deeply attended to someone else, that person is now inclined to attend to you and whatever input you offer. By listening so well, you will be listened to as well.

♥

Being willing to be a good and patient listener,
without trying to lead the communication, can make
it possible to move the conversation forward.

♥

Is it safe?

A little girl, with tears in her eyes, approached her daddy, one hand covering the other.

"Daddy, I have a splinter. But don't touch!"

"Okay, Nikki. Can I look if I promise not to touch?"

"You promise not to touch?"

"I promise."

"Okay, but just looking."

"I see it, Nikki. What do you want me to do?"

"It hurts, Daddy."

"Yes, it looks like it hurts."

"Daddy, I want you to fix it. But I don't want you to hurt me."

"I want to fix it for you, Nikki. It might hurt a little."

"Will you stop if I tell you to? Stop right away?"

"I promise to stop the instant that you tell me to."

"Okay."

As Daddy proceeded to attend to the splinter, Nikki told him to stop a half-dozen times in the first 4 minutes. Each time he heard the word stop, he stopped immediately. Each time he stopped, Nikki let him continue until the splinter was successfully removed, even though it did end up hurting some. At the end, although her finger hurt, Nikki hugged her dad.

Adam and Maria finished up a pleasant dinner and were cleaning up together. Conversation moved easily from the kids to the yard work to the friends who'd recently moved away. As they put the last of the dishes in the dishwasher, Adam turned away and said, "I don't want to hear any complaints about my weight tonight, Maria."

Maria, caught off guard by the comment, was about to defend her reasons for being concerned about his weight– his family history of diabetes, his own high cholesterol, his increasing complaints about back pain. Instead, she realized that she hadn't brought the topic up in weeks, let alone tonight. Unclear where his comment had come from, she wondered if it signified that he wanted to talk about this but was afraid. Unsure how to proceed, she bought some time simply by saying, "Okay," and letting the subject drop. Adam harrumphed and dropped the line of conversation that had never quite happened. Maria worried that she might have lost her chance to discuss this with Adam, but she held her tongue. Her intuition told her that he'd have to be the one to lead this topic, and then only when he was ready.

The next night, as they sat quietly reading after dinner, Adam said, "I got on the scale at work today. My weight's up."

Maria felt relief that he had once more brought up this sensitive topic. But she also felt panic. She knew that she had to say something, but she sensed that the moment was fragile. If she tried to lead him into a discussion about why he should lose weight, she was sure he'd just stop talking and she'd once more be considered the enemy on this topic. So she again tried to find her way by taking as neutral a posture as she could find.

"You sound concerned," she said.

"Well, I am. It's never been this high."

"Are you worried?"

"Jake down at work – he's 2 years younger than me– just had a heart attack."

"Oh, how scary."

"I think the joke's over. I have to stop eating like a kid. But it's hard."

"How can I help?"

"I don't know, but it's good to know that you're on my side."

As Nikki's daddy and Maria both figured out, sometimes the way to move things forward is by being willing to stand still for a while. When someone has a sensitive or painful issue to attend to, it can feel very scary. The scared person wants to know that it's safe to enter this territory fraught with anxiety. One of the best ways to increase a sense of safety is by increasing a sense of control. The scared person gets to feel in full control of how fast the procedure moves forward and in what direction. When the listener lets the person with the problem lead, it's a statement of support. It's like saying, "I'm here to back you up, but I won't make you go anywhere you're not ready to go."

At regular intervals, the person with the problem may need to reaffirm that the brakes work. Like Nikki repeatedly checking out the "stop" system with her daddy, the person with the problem may repeatedly challenge the listener in ways that make it difficult to maintain the patient posture. Each time the challenge is successfully met, the terrain feels safer, allowing additional movement toward problem-solving. To the degree that the alliance feels trustworthy, it feels safe to proceed in scary directions despite the anxiety.

Whatever challenges arise for two people, resolution is likely to be more successful when there's a clear sense of alliance. That clear sense is more likely to be achieved when pacing has been loving, patient, and respectful. Being able and willing to be a good and patient listener, without trying to lead the communication, can in fact make it possible to move the conversation forward.

♥

There can be a world of difference between
<u>transmission</u> and <u>reception</u>.

♥

Communication

"She keeps putting words in my mouth!"
"He never listens to a word I say!"
"I never meant that!"
"I never said any such thing!"

*T*hese statements all represent failures in communication and failures in relating. It's awfully frustrating when the people you most want to have understand you seem to be the very people apparently determined to misunderstand every word you say.

George Bernard Shaw said, "The single biggest problem in communication is the illusion that it has taken place."

There can be a difference (sometimes a world of difference) between *transmission* and *reception*. *Transmission* is the message that the speaker sends. *Reception* is the message that the listener hears. Each end of the communication will be influenced by, and can be distorted by, the needs and the experiences of the participants.

The purpose of communication is for meaning to be exchanged. Communication can only be considered successful if the sender's intended message has been accurately understood by the receiver. If a couple has a history of scrambled communications, then it is the responsibility of both partners to take the initiative to engage in a process that confirms successful communication.

No communication can be assumed to be successfully accomplished unless there has been some confirmation. Neither the sender nor the receiver can bear, or be assigned, sole responsibility for ensuring the adequacy of communication.

The sender must check with the receiver that the transmission was clear and understood as intended. The receiver must confirm that what was understood matches the sender's intentions.

It is not good enough to insist that your message was clear. Regardless of why, where, or how the message became distorted, the transmission must be modified to become clear to the listener. The listener retains responsibility for a commitment to understanding.

Perhaps the sender is using language that was commonly understood in her family of origin but which her partner doesn't always interpret accurately. Perhaps the receiver is so used to having to defend himself at work that he automatically hears an attack even in neutral words. We all come from our own experiences which have left us with expectations and sensitivities that may not be serving us well in this relationship place. It's important to use the right map for where you are Here and Now.

There's a simple but effective way to make sure that what you're sending is what's being received and that what you're hearing is the message that was intended.

> *I call this simple communication technique (which I've refined but did not originate):* **A-B-A.**
>
> **A** (the first speaker) sends a message to **B** (the listener). (*transmission*)
>
> **B** responds only by stating back to **A** the message that was understood. (*reception*)
>
> **A** then affirms that the reception was accurate or clarifies the transmission so that it's received accurately by **B**.
>
> This continues until **B** is clear on what **A** is saying and **A** is satisfied that **B** is hearing the intended message. Only then will **B** become the speaker and assume the role of **A**.

Here's a simple example of an **A-B-A** –

> **A** – "I'm sick and tired of cooking."
>
> **B** – "You're saying that you don't want to make dinner for me tonight."
>
> **A** – "Not exactly. I mean that I want to feel appreciated for the effort that I'm making to prepare a meal for you."
>
> **B** – "You're feeling unappreciated."
>
> **A** – "Yes, that's it."
>
> **B** – "I'm sorry that you feel that I took you for granted. Thank you for cooking. I do appreciate it."

This simple technique accomplishes several very important things. First, the sender learns right away that her original transmission was not clear. Regardless of why the message wasn't clear or where the message became distorted, the transmission must be modified to become clear to the listener. The speaker then has the opportunity and responsibility to rephrase the message until it captures the meaning that was intended (*transmission*). The message must also be in a form that the listener can understand (*reception*). This is true communication.

Second, the listener is required to listen carefully. Transmission may be futile if there's no commitment to reception. Without careful listening it'll be impossible to restate the message that was sent. Any failure to attend closely will be immediately apparent to the speaker. Also, if the original message was unclear, the listener has the immediate opportunity (and responsibility) to share that with the speaker. Then the message can be made clear. This demonstrates a commitment on the part of the listener to hear and understand the speaker's message and a commitment on the part of the speaker to be clear.

Both parties demonstrate a commitment to successful communication, which is also a commitment to the relationship.

As the example demonstrates, when an **A-B-A** takes place, the combination of clarified transmission and active listening tends to reveal not only the problem, but the solution as well.

Probably the most powerful aspect of **A-B-A** is that people feel listened to. When you feel listened to, you feel that someone is respecting and caring about what you think and feel. As soon as you feel that respect and caring, the interaction is no longer a fight. Now it's two people working together toward greater understanding. Hostility is reduced and closeness is increased.

When each partner in a relationship gets equal time to be **A**, then each partner can count on having his or her experience and feelings listened to and understood. This is one of the most powerful things that can occur between two people.

Once **A-B-A** becomes a habit, it can switch to a more natural way of partners checking in with each other to make sure that communication was successful on both ends. It can be, "this is what I understood you to say", or it could be, "did you really mean 'X'?, 'cuz that's what I heard."

The root of the word, "communication" is the same as the root of the word, "communion." It's derived from Latin and means "sharing in common". Successful communication is about two people sharing some meaning in common. It's about coming together.

Unsuccessful communication can drive people apart. Successful communication brings people closer.

♥

The best way to get someone to listen to your point of view
is to listen to theirs.

♥

Dead right

*W*ould you rather be right or be successful? In a relationship, each person walks in to any given situation believing, for the most part, that he or she is right. For each of us, there's a certain human reflex to defend our position. We believe that we have some reasonable justification for doing things as we are doing them. It makes sense to us after all. It can be a natural impulse to try to persuade our partner that what makes sense to us is therefore right. Well, remember the expression, "dead right"?

What if you're right but your partner is getting hurt or scared or angry because of what you're doing or how you're doing it? If that's not the outcome you were going for, then no matter how good, smart, sensible, etc., your reasons are for what you're doing, you're not being successful. Can you step out of this trap? Can you give up being right for the chance to be successful?

Perhaps you think that if you just explain it clearly enough, making especially clear how your partner is doing her part wrong or thinking his part wrong, then the obvious rightness of your way will be apparent. Can you possibly imagine that persuading anybody that he or she is wrong is a way to get closer?! If you alienate somebody, you might still be right, technically speaking, but you'll also be dead, figuratively speaking.

There's an alternative. One of the best ways to get someone to listen to your point of view is to listen to theirs. If there's a disagreement, you put yourself in a power position if you put aside any attempt to persuade and instead choose to listen to the opposition. Solicit the other person's thoughts and feelings. Ask, and be interested in the answer. This makes you look smart, since the other person thinks his or her answer is worth listening to. Now that you look smart and your partner feels that you've given due attention to his or her thoughts and feelings, your partner now is more open to hearing <u>your</u> thoughts and feelings. This is what you wanted in the first place. By giving up the need to be right, you've preserved your opportunity to be successful.

Once both partners' thoughts and feelings have been articulated, the next challenge presents itself. Assuming there is some divergence between the two positions, how do you proceed toward a successful outcome? It's possible that, having solicited and listened to your partner's thoughts, you now feel simply that your partner was right in the first place. Remember, successful trumps right every time. This is a fantastic opportunity to accede graciously to your partner's position, turning being wrong into being successful.

But maybe you still feel that your position has merit and are unwilling to give it up. This is no time to lose the success orientation. Prove once again how smart you are—ask your partner what he or she thinks might be a good way to resolve this divergence. Make clear that you seek an outcome that respects both perspectives. I guarantee that this makes you look smarter than declaring a unilaterally designed resolution, no matter how clever it might be. Listen carefully to the answer; ask questions until you really understand. Don't stop respectfully inquiring until you have a clear understanding of what's really important to your partner here. In most circumstances the two of you together can arrive at some resolution that is responsive to both parties' priorities.

The truth is that, in most cases, the process is more important than the outcome anyway. In the majority of circumstances, the process is successful when both parties feel properly respected and considered. It doesn't matter what the outcome is or how ultimately functional– if either party feels disrespected or disregarded, the process was a failure.

It's the process that defines whether the relationship is feeling good or bad. Keep your eye on the brass ring. Don't settle for being dead right when you can accomplish so much more.

♥

Once she felt listened to, she was willing
and able to listen to him.

♥

First, listen

Sean and Rosa were into a very familiar pattern. Convinced that Rosa did not fully understand his position, Sean was insisting that he needed to explain it to her again. Every time she opened her mouth to speak, he overrode her, speaking more loudly than she and insisting that she needed to understand his side of things.

Rosa was convinced that if only he listened to her he'd surely see her point. So she kept fending him off and trying to speak. When he got louder, she just waited him out, figuring that he'd have to take a breath eventually and that that would be her opportunity to make him hear her. She wasn't listening; she was just impatiently waiting her turn.

When he did pause and she did speak, it became obvious that she had been waiting to make a point but had not particularly listened to anything that he'd said. Frustrated by this, Sean waved away what she was trying to tell him and tried again to speak over her.

Each time, eventually, they both gave up and went their separate ways, convinced of the hopelessness of the effort. As such failures accumulated, they each tried less and less often to share feelings or thoughts of any consequence. The fabric of their relationship was getting thinner and thinner as time went on without substantive communication. Yet they both wished that something would happen that would make their futile, and increasingly rare, attempts at communication more satisfying and more productive.

Sean was the first one to undertake to change the way they communicated. He'd been participating in leadership training at work and figured that some of what he was learning might be useful at home. From his point of view, there HAD to be a better way than the way they'd been doing it.

In the training, the coach had been stressing that a good leader listened before he led, especially if he hoped to be followed. Sean had no desire to become a leader at home, but he thought that the principles still applied. He did want Rosa to follow him in the sense of paying attention to what he had to say.

When the next opportunity presented itself, he restrained his impulse to try to force Rosa to listen to him. Instead, he told her straight out that he wanted first to hear and to understand her side of things.

Rosa blinked several times while she attempted to shift gears. She'd already been digging in her heels and this threw her for a loop. Afraid to lose the moment, she collected herself and started talking. She spoke quickly in hopes of getting it all out before he changed his mind. To her surprise, he listened without interruption. When she was finished, he asked her a couple of questions in an effort to understand more fully what she had told him. He listened again to her answers.

It was only after that that he undertook to present his point of view. Furthermore, because he'd listened to her, his own perspective now reflected his understanding of her perspective.

Rosa was ready to jump in and shout him down, but there was no need. He seemed to have listened without the need for her to do any shouting. Because of his patient and active listening, she felt that he'd been authentically committed to understanding her point of view. Once she felt that she'd been truly listened to by someone who really wanted to know her thoughts and feelings, she was much more willing and able to listen to his. With his demonstration of listening, she felt that he'd shown commitment both to understanding her message and to their relationship. His point of view was now something to which she could attend without defensiveness. Without having to fight for her right to be heard, she was much more accessible as a listener. She copied what he had done—listening attentively, without interruption, then asking questions to clarify what she'd heard, and then listening to his answers. Feeling his commitment to understand her thoughts and feelings, she felt very close to him and eager to hear and understand his thoughts and feelings too. The result was not only a successful communication but a nourished relationship.

♥

As the competition wears on,
neither partner gets what he or she was seeking.

♥

Competitive suffering –
the game that everybody loses

*P*enny came home from work and walked into the kitchen, where Nino was chopping vegetables for dinner. She sank into a chair, groaning, and said, "What an awful day!"

Nino continued to chop as he said, "You think you've had a lousy day! I had to fire that awful accounting clerk, hire a temp to do the payroll, and deal with the union over the firing."

Let's talk about what went wrong here and is about to go even worse. Penny entered the situation with a presentation that was seeking sympathy and inquiry. She wanted Nino to sympathize with her obvious distress and to ask her about what had caused it. That implicit request was ignored (or rejected)—he did neither thing.

Nino presented with his own distress, for which he also obviously wanted sympathy. It seems likely that his day did deserve sympathy. But because of his offhanded rejection of Penny's request, he made it unlikely that her first impulse would be sympathetic. She felt that he ignored her feelings and carelessly defined them as less important than his. Instead of sympathetic, she was hurt and angry. She didn't get what she wanted here, and he's not going to get what he wants either.

In order to get the comfort that she was seeking, Penny now believes that she has to persuade Nino that <u>his</u> day wasn't as bad as <u>hers</u>. Instead of making solicitous inquiries about the difficult events of his day, she'll now tell him about the details of her suffering. Nino will, of course, receive this as rejecting his overture requesting understanding and sympathy. In an effort to drag the sympathy wagon back to <u>his</u> day, he'll now try to trump her overture with more evidence that clearly demonstrates why his day was more deserving of sympathy. He might give more details about his events; or he might knit himself a noose by explaining to her why her details were really not so bad. The first direction is rejecting; the second is insulting. Neither one will be successful in getting him what he really wants (but the second is lethal).

As the competition wears on, neither partner is getting what he or she was seeking. Unfortunately, as the contest continues, it becomes <u>less</u> likely that it can have any kind of successful or gratifying outcome for either party. The accumulation of hurt and angry feelings has no potential to lead to a happy resolution. Bottom-line—you can't win this contest. And the more you play, the more you lose.

But there is a way to have that ever-desirable win-win. Since Penny spoke first, Nino had the opportunity to increase the likelihood that he'd get the sympathy he wanted by first giving her the sympathy that she was seeking. By being willing to contain his own need <u>temporarily</u>, he could improve the odds that his need would be met and met satisfactorily. When he restrains his own impulse to share his distress, he can offer sympathy and inquiry to Penny. When she feels that he has listened to, understood, and responded to <u>her</u> need, then she is in the perfect place to be able to offer to him the sympathy and inquiry that he is looking for. She feels respected and cared about – the very feelings that prepare her to reciprocate to him.

Once her day's wounds are bound, she can breathe out and turn toward him with all the inquiry that he wishes, asking about his day with authentic interest. At that point, instead of him having to defeat her in the futile hope of getting his needs met, she'll be the willing bearer of loving feelings. They'll both get taken care of and no blood will be shed. The relationship will have been nourished by the generosity of their responsiveness to each other. Instead of a mutual loss, it's a gain for both parties and for the relationship.

♥

The goal is to have everybody feel listened to and considered.

♥

Family meeting

*D*ixie, the 12 year old, wanted Disney World. Davis, the 15 year old, wanted to ski. Dora, the mom, wanted a quiet beach. And Drew, the dad, wanted a decision. He personally tended to favor camping; but he was more interested in a decision that he could act on than getting his preferred destination.

For weeks now they'd been living in a swirl of brochures, maps, and glossy photos of vacation destinations. Each one of his family members was lobbying for his or her dream vacation. Finally Drew couldn't stand it any longer. He just wanted a decision made and demanded that they come to some conclusion by the end of the weekend.

Dora suggested that they have a family meeting to address the issue. As they gathered around the dining room table that evening, Dora, Dixie, and Davis all arrived toting piles of marketing information to help them make their cases. Drew groaned as he saw the potential for hours of arguing.

He took command of the meeting and suggested that they compromise on a camping vacation, since they'd always enjoyed them in the past. The howls of outrage made him retreat instantly. But it was too late. Once he'd made his suggestion, the floodgates opened – each one leaped forward and tried to make his or her case, which provoked each other family member to protest on one or another grounds. The voices got louder and the protests more impassioned. No one was really listening to anyone else at that point.

Drew couldn't stand the disorderly process and finally banged on the table with his crab mallet.

"Enough! We're going to go to the beach, and that's final. This meeting is over." He banged the mallet one more time and walked away from the table. He was relieved that the decision was made and proud that he could be the one to bring efficiency to the family meeting process.

Dixie ran to her room and cried. Davis slouched off to his room grumbling about fascists and turned his music up loud. Dora followed Drew out of the room and confronted him as he was sitting down in front of the TV.

Before she could speak, Drew smiled and said, "Don't thank me. It's all part of the service I perform around here to make these things go more efficiently. I figured no one was more deserving of having her choice of vacation than you, Dora."

Instead of thanking him, she snarled at him that he was a tyrannical, dictatorial, overbearing bully and that she'd rather vacation in a leper colony than go to the beach with him.

Once he recovered and could speak, he insisted that his behavior had been the only logical way to an efficient resolution of the vacation problem.

After taking a long, deep breath to calm herself, Dora tried to explain that family process wasn't about efficiency. She explained that family process had to respect every member's feelings and needs, and not just achieve a decision about a vacation destination. The goal was to have everybody feel listened to and considered. Obviously not everybody's wishes were going to be fulfilled every time. But everybody had to feel that his or her wishes were authentically listened to and considered. That wasn't inherently a very efficient process, she acknowledged. The ultimate achievement wasn't any particular decision; it was a family that worked together in respectful and productive ways. She pointed out that it was the same between just the two of them—they'd always tried to make it a process where they both felt listened to and respected.

After a little time to reflect on what Dora had said, Drew called a family meeting for the next night. He asked each person to present, in five minutes or less, why they wanted their particular vacation. He enforced a rule that for those five minutes no one else could speak other than to ask a reasonable and relevant question. At the end of all of the presentations, he asked for suggestions of how they could best achieve a compromise that was responsive to each person's wishes.

It knocked his socks off when the kids themselves came up with a very creative and responsive solution. Davis said he'd be happy to water ski instead of snow ski; Dixie said that she'd find a beach resort within driving distance of Disney World that offered water sports as part of a family vacation package.

Drew got his reward early when Dora came around the table after the meeting and hugged him and told him how much she loved him for being able to listen instead of take charge. He felt like quite the winner even though there was no camping on the vacation horizon.

Although not necessarily the speediest way to a conclusion, this highly respectful process provided not only a resolution to the vacation question but also strengthened the fabric of this family's relationships. With each person feeling listened to, each person felt respected and loved. The vacation brought this family closer together even before it began.

♥

The listener's true responsibility is to listen.

♥

Mirror, mirror on the wall–
reflection as a communication strategy

*T*here's an amusing T-shirt that I've seen around lately. It says, "My wife says I never listen to her. At least that's what I think she said." As such shirts are meant to do, it gets a chuckle as we recognize a nearly universal accusation – "you're not listening to me!"

Although the shirt is amusing, the experience is not. No one likes to feel that the things that they felt were worth saying someone else felt were not worth listening to. The other side of the coin is no fun either – if you <u>are</u> paying attention and your partner gives you no credit for it. But, of course, there's a solution.

There's a communication strategy called "Reflection". This is an extension and elaboration of the **A-B-A** exercise. To review, a listener says back to the speaker what the speaker just said, but in the listener's own words. The listener is saying to the speaker just what meaning the listener took from the speaker's words. If the reception, or "reflection", matches the speaker's intended message, then the speaker continues. If the reception is a distortion of the intended message and not an accurate reflection, then the speaker must stop and clarify the intended message. This reflection and clarification process continues until the speaker is confident that the listener has accurately understood the intended message.

As with any good mirror, nothing is brought by the receiver other than what's introduced by the speaker. The listener's own ideas, thoughts, and feelings are put on hold during this piece of interaction. Obviously the full range of communication cannot be accomplished in a one-sided format like this. But for this piece of the communication puzzle, the listener functions strictly as a mirror.

There are several advantages to this format for both speaker and listener. The speaker has the listener's commitment to be an active listener, as opposed to the listener being casually present and more or less inattentive. Obviously, any failure to attend carefully to the speaker's words will be revealed in a failure to reflect accurately. This commitment to active listening is frequently the key ingredient in re-establishing friendly relations. When someone feels that you care enough to commit your time and energy to listening, they feel supported, cared about, and energized.

For the listener, there are also advantages, even beyond the achievement of those good feelings in the speaker. For the listener, this is an opportunity to put aside any responsibility to clarify, educate, or defend your own position. At this point you have no need to make your own stuff "win" any kind of battle against your partner's stuff. You're also relieved of any responsibility to "fix" your partner's stuff. You don't have to problem-solve or rescue. You can just kick back and be off the hook. All you have to do is listen carefully.

Listeners sometimes feel guilty initially that they aren't "doing" more. Especially when a problem is being presented, active listening and reflection sometimes makes people feel that they aren't doing their jobs if they haven't solved the problem by the end of the conversation. What's being overlooked here is that the listener's true responsibility is to listen. When people want problem solving, they'll ask for it directly. But much of the time what people want is to be listened to, truly listened to. It happens so rarely for most of us that when it does occur, it's a very powerful experience.

People who are new at this sometimes ask, "What do I say?" In fact, that's the easy part. All the material you need is presented by the speaker. You're doing it just right if you don't bring anything in that wasn't introduced by the speaker. Here's an example of a good reflection–

SPEAKER: That @#*#@ manager left the disaster in my lap again.

LISTENER: It sounds like you're angry that you've been left with clean-up again.

SPEAKER: It's not like he leaves me the resources to fix it.

LISTENER:Are you concerned that you don't have the resources you need to solve the problem this time?

SPEAKER: Yeah, but I'll scrabble up something, like always.

LISTENER: Yeah, you always work something out.

This reflection worked well because the listener remained in the listener role. There was no attempt to take over the role of director or savior. The speaker ended up feeling supported during stress and affirmed during solution. The listener refrained from trying to evaluate the problem or to develop an action plan. The speaker retained ownership and could end the conversation also owning the solution. The role that the listener could properly contribute – empathy, support, affirmation – was carried out well. People are often surprised at how easy it is to be successful once you focus only on listening and put any other agenda aside.

Mirror, mirror on the wall   successful communication doesn't need to be a fairy tale.

♥

The true goal of communication is
the ultimate survival of all points of view.

♥

Communication, not combat

"*I*t feels like one continuous power struggle between us."
"It doesn't seem to matter what the issue is –
it's always about who's going to win and who's going to lose."
"She always has to have her way."
"Hey, you can only push me so far. Then I push back, hard."
Sound familiar? It too often happens that in the very relationships where you expect people to come together, things break down instead into opposition or warfare.

We hope and expect that the people who care about us will see things the way we do. But sometimes two separate people will have two different perspectives. Each one sees the obvious rightness of his or her own position. Each one expects the other also to see that same obvious rightness.

It's always uncomfortable to discover that someone close to you doesn't see things your way. To make matters worse, the other person expects you to see things their way. That feels like a challenge not only to how you see things but perhaps also to your place in the relationship. You wonder if there's room in the relationship for only one person's perspective, one definition of truth. Like many people, you may respond by aggressively making it clear that you carry substantial weight in this relationship and that you'll only accept unconditional surrender to your position. So what started out with the intention of sharing a point of view turns into what feels like a battle for survival.

The will to survive is a good thing and most healthy creatures will feel motivated to ensure their own survival. The problem comes from the mistaken belief that your survival is best ensured through the other person's failure to survive. Of course, in the average conversation actual survival is not at stake. It's more a case of having your point of view survive by slaying the opponent's point of view. But this too is a miscalculation. In fact, in a relationship, the true goal of communication is the ultimate survival of *all* points of view. Successful communication means that everyone's point of view gets understood by all participants. Understood does not necessarily mean agreed with. In a relationship, one of the most basic needs of those involved is to feel that their experience is listened to, understood, and respected by their partner.

In fact, whenever you feel that you have been listened to, understood, and respected, you feel that your place in the relationship is recognized, your point of view is granted its due space. When you feel this kind of security, you don't feel the need to fight. If you don't have to fight, then you don't have to win, and someone else doesn't have to lose. At that point there's room for multiple and diverse points of view.

Sometimes partners get into a habit of drifting into a fight when what they were aiming for was a conversation. It can happen insidiously, without apparent warning or intention. I've developed a technique that can alert you, in a non-verbal way, when the effort toward communication is breaking down and this survival defense is starting to kick in. This awareness allows you to act early to get the conversation (and relationship) back on track.

I call this technique, "hand-to-hand non-combat". Two people sit facing each other across a table – one person with right elbow resting on the table, right forearm and hand up, while the other person has the left elbow resting on the table, left forearm and hand up. Their hands meet palm to palm. While holding this position, they discuss some issue of concern to them. If at any time a power struggle is beginning to sneak into the conversation, it will quickly be revealed by one partner starting to push against the other's hand.

Remember, the power struggle <u>follows</u> a sense that one's perspective isn't being considered and that therefore one's right to space in the relationship is in jeopardy. This can be addressed at the moment when the defensive pressure is first noticed. By directing attention to the underlying feelings, the more basic issues between people can be addressed, negotiated, and resolved. Instead of the same old power struggle happening, it becomes an opportunity to help each partner feel that his or her experience is being recognized and will be listened to, understood, and respected. Then true communication can occur and power struggles are unnecessary.

People don't truly need their partners always to agree with them. But they do need to feel that they've been listened to, understood, and respected. And when they don't, you'll feel the pressure.

♥

Communication can only take place if both
listener and speaker feel safe.

♥

Creating a safe space

*I*n order for successful listening to take place, it is necessary for both parties to the communication to feel that it is safe both to *speak authentically* and to *listen undefensively.*

If an honest and non-offensive expression is met with a punitive response instead of receptiveness, expression will not continue and communication will not take place. As the listener, you will leave the interaction without the input that you need in order to understand your partner.

Similarly, if a transmission is made with hostility or accusation or any other hurtful attitude, the listener will reflexively assume a defensive posture. A defensive posture cannot, by definition, be open and receptive. As a speaker you will leave the interaction without being understood or responded to because the nature of your transmission shut down the communication process.

Communication can only take place successfully if both listener and speaker feel safe.

It is the speaker's responsibility to ensure that the transmission is delivered clearly, authentically, and non-offensively. Any suggestion of aggression is likely to shut down the process.

It is the listener's responsibility to respond to such an honorable transmission by remaining receptive in service of understanding. This receptiveness is required even if the transmission is not what the listener wants to hear.

If you want to be heard, you must create and sustain an environment in which it is safe to listen to you.

If you want your partner to express authentically, you must make it safe for him or her to speak without fear of retribution.

♥

Aggression makes us feel individually powerful,
but the relationship cost is high.

♥

Aggression as self-protection

*I*t turned out to be one of their ugliest fights ever. She was really upset about something that he'd done and was telling him very clearly how hurt and angry she was. He seemed to be listening. He even looked ashamed of what he'd done. She was floored when what she thought was going to be an apology turned into a blistering attack. Somehow, instead of saying that he was sorry, now he was screaming at her about how the whole thing was her fault. Her every deficiency was listed in graphic detail and how it caused him to behave the way that he had.

She fled the room. Not only did it feel hopeless to talk to him, it had become scary. He had achieved a depth of meanness that made it impossible to feel safe in a conversation with him.

After she left the room, he had a brief surge of triumph. He felt big and powerful. It was rapidly replaced with a feeling of shame and loneliness. This was a woman, after all, whom he'd protect without hesitation from anyone who dared to harm or frighten her. This was the woman he loved. How could he be the one to hurt her so badly? The look in her eyes when she'd run from the room cut him to the heart.

He stood up and moved toward the bedroom, a sincere apology on his lips. But then he remembered the feeling of shame when she'd confronted him with what he'd done. His stomach sank and he stopped moving toward her. He couldn't bear to feel that shame again. It made him feel so small and weak. He couldn't, he wouldn't willingly feel that again. He turned away from the bedroom and walked instead into his den and sat down at his desk. He buried himself in paperwork; and he pushed away the image of her face in tears. When it intruded, he reminded himself that it was her fault this had happened in the first place.

For several days after that, she left him pretty much alone. They behaved civilly in front of the kids and other people; but they never discussed anything of consequence. He occasionally caught her crying when she thought she was alone in the house. He wanted so much to comfort her, but he couldn't bring himself to talk about what had happened.

Needing to talk to someone, he finally confided in a woman friend at work whom he'd known for years. He was disappointed but not surprised when she told him that he'd been a jerk. Hoping that he could change her assessment with more explanation, he tried to clarify how this was really his wife's fault. His colleague wasn't buying it. Worse, she pointed out that every time he started to accept his proper responsibility in the whole event, he would rapidly digress into blaming his wife.

But she also gave him a life ring to grab onto. She pointed out that the fact that he was talking to her about this demonstrated that he was troubled by the whole thing. Much as he couldn't seem to stay with his own culpability, he did in fact recognize, however fleetingly, that he needed to accept responsibility for his own poor behavior. He really did recognize that he was hurting someone that he was sworn to protect and he did not like the feeling that he was failing her.

He was now feeling more uncomfortable from the shame of failing her than from the shame of being wrong. He was an inherently honest man, so he admitted to himself that his friend was right—he had been a jerk. He wondered if he had the guts to admit it to his wife. He had no particular confidence right now that she'd accept even an apology from him. He wasn't sure that he could stay an honorable course if she started attacking him, no matter how much it might be deserved.

He was pretty sure that he was ready and able to walk into the lion's den; but he wasn't sure that once there he'd remain able to put aside his aggression-as-protection. He figured he'd need courage and faith in his marriage to carry this off without bloodshed. He told himself that he'd done other things in his life that scared him — he'd been in combat, for heaven's sake. He'd done that because he believed in the cause for which he was fighting. Well, he believed in his marriage and in his love for his wife. He could do this too. He walked into the house determined to behave in a way that he could respect. He was committed to find the strength to face her feelings and his own guilt and shame.

Shame, guilt, regret, someone else's rage—these are all things that can make us feel small, helpless, weak, or defensive. Those are very uncomfortable feelings. We tend to feel highly motivated to make those feelings go away, fast. Unfortunately, one of the most efficient ways of doing that is to take the offensive and take cover in our own rage and attacking behavior. That makes us feel individually powerful instead of weak, but the cost to the relationship is high.

She saw something different in his eyes when he approached her this time. Although she felt uneasy about having a substantive conversation with him, she chose to hear him out. When he demonstrated no aggression at all and made no attempt to defend his previous behavior, she started to relax and feel more able to participate in the conversation. Wisely, she chose to focus on her hurt rather than attacking him for his behavior during that awful event.

It was a long time before she felt really safe talking to him about emotionally charged issues. It was longer still before she felt really safe expressing authentically when she was angry about something. They kept working at it, gradually establishing a sense of safety together.

♥

War is what you settle for when you
can't get the loving peace.

♥

When war seems safer than love

*P*eople walk into relationships with the hope and expectation that they will find a kind of sanctuary. The partner is a bulwark against the cold, cruel world outside the relationship. The image of the relationship is that of a place of acceptance, validation, comfort, and trust. It's a castle fortified against the slings and arrows of the outside world.

It sometimes happens that, over the course of time, events accumulate where the partnership fails, in ways large or small, or both, to live up to that image. At some point, that accumulation may overwhelm a person's ability to trust and feel that it's safe to remain vulnerable in the relationship.

It is at that point that a person may begin to see a partner not as a perfect ally but instead as an enemy, someone against whom one must defend oneself. The person whom you'd believed you could trust above all others is now someone who can't be trusted. The lover has become the enemy. The flip from *alliance with* to *defense against* can be particularly violent when it follows the disappointment of losing a lover.

The pain of that perceived loss can be huge; and pain can lead directly to rage. At that point, it seems logical, even righteous, to mount an angry and vigorous war against a previously beloved partner.

However cold, lonely, and painful the war may be, it can feel like a safer choice than the vulnerability that goes with hoping and trying to be loved in a situation in which that love no longer feels secure, consistent, or solid. People can only remain in such an insecure position for so long before it becomes too scary to sustain. At that point war seems safer than a vulnerable peace.

As happens with nations as well, once one party goes for war, it's really hard for the other party to remain in a peaceful and positive posture. It seems only logical and sensible at that point to take a comparably cold and angry posture, to meet each assault with either offense or defense. It takes tremendous courage and vision to meet anger with an affirmation of love.

Paradoxically, that in fact is exactly what's being sought. The wounded partner does not truly wish for war. The wish is for the sanctuary relationship. In relationships, war is only what you settle for when you can't get the loving peace that you crave. War isn't a first choice; it's what you resort to when you think you can't have, safely, what you really want with your partner.

It's easy to fight aggression or anger with aggression and anger. It's really hard to meet that aggression and anger with an effort to reestablish the original loving peace.

Generally, the original alliance came to be for some powerful and meaningful reasons. In most cases those reasons didn't go away. They got buried under an accumulation of hurts and disappointments. Sometimes those wounds can't be recovered from and are fatal to a relationship. More often it takes individual courage and faith in the relationship to create out of a war an opportunity for healing and reconstruction.

♥

Shifting the rules of engagement from
"shoot to kill" to "listen to learn".

♥

Hold your fire!

When Mike and Sandy sat down for their first counseling session as a couple, the air around them was charged. Sandy
was sitting with every muscle clenched and a set look to her jaw
that suggested that she was more than ready to rumble. She sat
turned rigidly away from Mike. Mike, in contrast, seemed to be willfully assuming a posture with neither offense nor even defense.
His body language was suggesting that he was open and ready
but with no aggression – his arms were at his sides, his legs were
uncrossed, his body was turned toward Sandy, his eyes met hers
whenever she turned stiffly toward him.

Mike invited Sandy to speak first, but she just shook her head
angrily and refused to speak. Mike opened in a strong, even voice
with a statement of love for Sandy, commitment to his marriage,
and a willingness to do whatever was necessary to make things
work for them together.

That was all it took to trigger an onslaught from Sandy. She
proceeded to develop an extensive list of Mike's failings and faults
that reached 12 years back. Mike found a source of courage and
strength inside himself at that moment and chose not to defend
himself against any of the accusations. He didn't even change
posture in his chair except to lean forward to listen carefully to
everything she said. When she came up for air, he once again
stated his absolute commitment to do whatever was necessary for
her and for their marriage.

Sandy had been ready for a down and dirty exchange of accusations and defenses – she was revved for it. It was that very rev
that was insulating her at that moment from feeling her real connection to Mike and was thereby allowing her to see him simply

as the enemy. If Mike had taken the expected line of defense and participated in this battle with her, they could each have armored themselves against a bond that had grown over many years together. In the name of personal defense, they could have set themselves on a course of mutually assured destruction. However strong and gratifying this might have appeared in the short term, the end result would have been a marriage in ruins and each of them carrying immense battle scars and losses.

By proactively choosing to stay focused on his love for Sandy and his wish to stay married to her, Mike was able to keep his own impulse to protect himself from taking over and leading him in a direction that would have proved counterproductive. His capacity for "holding fire" was admirable, but it was also just plain effective. When he didn't shoot back, he essentially shifted the rules of engagement from "shoot to kill" to "listen to learn".

When Mike didn't fight back, Sandy was rendered vulnerable once more to her deep connection to Mike. Her furious energy dissipated when it wasn't fed by rage from Mike. She didn't want any more simply to hurt someone who had hurt or disappointed her. Now her more important agenda resurfaced – she wanted Mike to understand and care about her needs so that she could receive from him those things that she'd been missing. With Mike persistently remaining in a receptive posture, Sandy began to believe that perhaps what she really wanted to build with Mike might be possible. If that were so, then maybe she didn't have to settle for destruction.

Truth is, most people set themselves a course of burn-and-slash only after they fear that love-and-build isn't available to them in a reliable way. When a partner responds to attack with attack, the person who began the fight is only reinforced in believing that destruction is what the relationship is all about now. When, as with Mike, there isn't a return attack, then the attacking partner is invited to reconsider the status of the relationship. It's as if to say, "Hey, whoa, that direction isn't my choice. I choose to make love, not war. Interested?"

It isn't always easy to resist the impulse to protect yourself by hitting back. But no one's really safe in a war. You can choose to try to change the rules of engagement. If your partner is set on a course of destruction, you may not be able to change that. But holding fire may open up other possibilities, possibilities that may serve you better in the long run. Have you the courage not to fight?

♥

Feeling understood is a powerful
binding force between people.

♥

Understanding

As soon as we are born, we are separate. It's wonderful to be a separate person, an individual, each with a unique experience. It's also hard – your wonderfully unique experience, while a treasure, is also something that isolates you from another person, whose experience is unique to <u>him</u>. No two people experience the universe in quite the same way. And while this is infinitely fertile and rich for the world, it also contributes to a feeling of aloneness for each individual.

One of the ways that we seek to bridge the gulf between us and another human being is by feeling understood by the other person. We each want to feel known and understood. We crave it. It helps us to feel connected to another human spirit. It also helps us feel validated. If we are understood, then we are understandable. We make sense to another person. We are, in some way, a part of the greater whole. We are separate but not alone.

It can be difficult to bridge the gap between people. Each person, experiencing the universe in a unique way, develops a unique perspective. No two perspectives are exactly alike. Being human, we tend to believe however that everyone is likely to perceive things as we perceive them. And if they don't, well, they're wrong. Within a relationship, it seems all the more likely that someone to whom you're close will see things as you see them. Of course, that often works out to be true, since we tend to choose people who are essentially like-minded. When someone to whom you're close has a widely divergent perception from yours, it can feel very confusing, even anxiety provoking. It tends to create a feeling again of disconnection.

The best way to address such a moment of disconnection is likely to be communication. If you can understand how and why your partner perceives as he or she does, if you can communicate to your partner so that he or she understands how or why YOU perceive as you do, then the likely result is communion instead of disconnection.

Feeling understood is a powerful binding force between people.

♥

Neither one recognizes that the problem
lies in a difference of perspective.

♥

The care and feeding of a marriage

Will had his arms crossed tightly across his chest, and his jaw was set in a hard line. Kate had asked for more demonstrations of affection – spontaneous gestures like hugs, handholding, anniversary cards. Will was insistent that Kate knew that he loved her and so these gestures were unnecessary. For 12 years together he'd never cheated on her, never beaten her, gone to work every day to earn money to support the family, come home every evening.

Will said, "I took those vows 12 years ago and I meant them. She has never had any reason to doubt that. This is all just nonsense!"

Kate couldn't seem to make up her mind whether to throw up her hands in disgust, slug him, or cry.

I asked Kate to stop and notice the content of Will's message – that he loved her, and had loved her with a constancy that had endured 12 years. She stopped wanting to slug him; and she didn't feel particularly disgusted. But she still seemed tearful.

"Then why won't he do these things that let me know he feels that way? What's the big deal?"

This is a common situation – here are two people who experience something very differently. Neither one recognizes that the problem lies in a difference of perspective. He feels she's complaining about something without any merit. She feels he's withholding something out of meanness or indifference.

The truth is that he doesn't understand her need for these gestures of affection. If he understood it, he'd want to meet that need, just as he's always tried to meet every need of hers since he first fell in love with her. What he understands is that his best efforts to be a good husband aren't cutting it. He's feeling that all the big things, like 12 years of faithfulness, don't count with her.

Because it's obvious to her how important these small gestures of affection are, she expects it to be obvious to him. If it's obvious to him and he still doesn't do it, then she fears that it must be because he doesn't want to be loving to her. At this point she's not only missing the affectionate gestures, but she's also hurt because she thinks that he's willfully depriving her of something he must know that she wants.

This is a great set-up for very hurt feelings on both sides. But it's essentially a case of misunderstanding between two people who love each other. It's the very fact that they love each other that makes them both vulnerable to being hurt.

Will sees his marriage vows as a promise to Kate that's active each and every day. He knows that he lives for her. Nothing is as important to him as taking care of Kate. He believes that he demonstrates it every time he goes to work when he'd rather go fishing. He sees fidelity as a statement of his enduring love for her. It looks to him like she's dismissing it as a trivial gesture, less important than an anniversary card.

Kate looks around her and sees that people change, relationships change, over the course of years. She's seen many of her friends go through divorces after 5, 10, even 20 years of marriage. She knows that she loves Will. She knows that he's a very responsible man who believes in keeping promises. That doesn't address her ongoing need to feel in tangible ways that he stays with her not because he should but because he loves her and cares about her feelings.

As Will and Kate continued to share their feelings, each came to understand the other person's emotional experience. Because they truly did love each other, it wasn't particularly difficult for either of them to make the efforts required to let their partner <u>feel</u> loved. As Will came to understand Kate's need for demonstrations of affection as well as her love for him, it gave him great pleasure to bring her happiness with hugs, kisses, and cards. As Kate felt loved and taken care of, it became easier to express to Will her appreciation for his efforts, whether for going to work every day or for the hugs and kisses.

The next task for them as a couple was to keep the process alive. One of the best ways to do this is to engage in special rituals together that explicitly declare love and devotion. One popular variation is taking marriage vows again to mark an anniversary, whether it's the second, the tenth, or each anniversary. Second honeymoons (or third, or fourth) can be a lovely opportunity to demonstrate commitment and to share joy. On a smaller scale, setting aside an evening together every week (or every month, if that's the best you can manage) both demonstrates commitment and provides opportunity for sharing and closeness. Unless time is made for sharing, the kinds of misunderstandings that Will and Kate experienced occur too easily and too often.

♥

Inquiry says that your partner cares about you
enough to want to understand.

♥

Inquiry—a step toward understanding

*P*eople consistently overestimate how well they know their partners. Game shows regularly demonstrate, in the most humiliat-
ing ways imaginable, that people don't know their partners nearly
as well as they think they do.

It is tremendously seductive to believe that because you
know someone well, and/or for a long time, that you can know
what they're feeling or thinking or wanting at any given moment.
Sometimes it's a question of projecting our own thoughts and feelings onto someone else. Sometimes it's a question of misreading
signals. Sometimes it's just not knowing some critical bit of history that would make things make sense. However it happens, we
often find ourselves in a position of believing we know something
that we do not.

Recognizing how important it is for a partner to feel known and
understood, it behooves us to take the necessary steps to understand accurately. Knowing how powerful an experience it is for a
person to feel understood, it is a poor choice to give in to impulse,
or egocentrism, or even imagination instead of finding out for real
what our partners are thinking, feeling, and needing. "For real"
has to mean that even when our partner's feelings are different
from our own, even if they're puzzling or confusing or troubling, we
remain committed to understanding.

It is a potent demonstration of commitment when a partner
takes a posture of authentic inquiry, even when the thoughts and
feelings are unexpected or hard to understand or hard to hear.
The message is one of affirmation and elevation. It says that your
partner cares about you enough to want to understand. Asking
reflects a willingness on the other person's part to put aside his

or her own thoughts and feelings and history in service of understanding yours. It's a demonstration of selflessness. That is a powerful message for one partner to give another. It's a message that contributes significantly to feeling secure and respected in the relationship.

♥

Don't confuse a guess, even one based
on experience, with knowing.

♥

Ask!

"I thought you preferred me blonde."
"What do you mean— you don't want children?"
"I thought you'd be upset if I took the transfer, so I said 'no' ".

You know the old joke about what happens when you **ASSUME**? It makes an **ASS** of **U** and **ME**. Well, old joke or not, there's a timely lesson to be learned. It applies particularly to what happens between partners, sometimes in small ways, sometimes in very important ways.

The longer that you know someone the more likely you are to believe that you can predict their responses. When you have an accumulation of experience with someone you tend to believe that this will allow you to guess accurately what that person's thoughts and feelings will be. You may indeed guess accurately sometimes, further leading you to believe that your powers of prediction are more perfectly accurate than they in fact are. Even the best guesser is still playing the odds, not working from the facts. No matter how well you think that you know someone, you can only work from your best guess about what they're thinking or feeling. Don't confuse a guess, even one based on history and observation, with knowing.

The problem arises when your behavior is based on your predictions instead of on the other person's true thoughts and feelings. This can become a problem when you lose sight of the possibility of a difference between your predictions and the other person's actual thoughts and feelings.

For example, every night Cindy actively protected her husband, Sam, from being "bothered" by their son's requests for help with homework. She'd drop whatever she was doing to help with the day's assignments. One evening, when she had to be away from home, Sam helped out with the homework. The next day he commented on how good it felt to be able to help his son. Cindy was dumbfounded. She felt angry and foolish. Why hadn't he told her?! His answer – "You never asked."

It turned out that Cindy had grown up in a household where her father insisted on only the most remote involvement in his children's daily lives. He required that his wife intercede to prevent any demands on his evening. Cindy had assumed that the father of her child would feel the same way. She then behaved in a way that fit her assumptions but which didn't in fact fit her husband's real wishes or needs. She felt overtaxed and resentful every night about a "rule" that did not in reality exist.

Sam, on the other hand, thought that Cindy was keeping herself between him and his son because she thought Sam was incompetent to help with schoolwork. He'd been hurt and defensive every night, just the way he'd felt when his first wife had criticized his every move. He'd assumed that Cindy was demonstrating her low opinion of him, just like his first wife. Cindy was offended and surprised to hear this. "Why did you assume that I was just like her? Why didn't you ask what I was thinking?"

Sometimes we get so caught up in our belief that we <u>know</u> that we neglect to check in on reality and match our beliefs to the facts. Our partners need and deserve to have our responses based on the facts. It's a most respectful gesture to ask your partner what he or she is in fact thinking and feeling, to ask how to interpret a particular behavior. Asking demonstrates caring and sensitivity. Asking also protects you from limiting yourself to the behaviors that you believe, perhaps inaccurately, are necessary or appropriate. There may be a whole range of possibilities available to you that you don't even know about because you're working from an inaccurate guidebook, one based not on current facts but on old baggage, misperceptions, or anxieties.

When asking is a sincere effort to understand, your partner feels gratified by your commitment to the relationship. This creates an opportunity for sharing. Assuming, on the other hand, leaves unexplored space between people. If the beliefs are too far from the facts, then assuming tends to make distance between people in place of closeness.

So, contrary to the military's former policy, do ask, do tell. You owe it to yourself and to your partner. Your relationship will be much richer for the sharing.

♥

Asking is an affirmation of commitment and caring.

♥

It's not about you

*I*t often happens that people believe that they are the targets
of their partners' anger or unhappiness when in fact they are
closer to being the solution than to being the problem.

Milton asked Charlene what she wanted for dinner and got
a very curt, "I'm not hungry," as a reply. He asked her how her
day was and got, "Long," as an answer. She slammed the kitchen
drawers closed as she put away the silverware from the dishwasher. Milton asked if she'd spoken to the painters and heard
a quick curse and, "I forgot to call them," as she walked to the
phone.

Milton figured he must be in trouble with Charlene. He was not
enthusiastic about finding out why, so he just quietly went to his
study and started doing the work waiting for him on his desk.

Interestingly, Milton had not been in trouble with Charlene until
he went off to his desk. He had been correct in recognizing her
bad mood but completely incorrect in interpreting its cause. In
fact, Charlene had been mad at pretty much everybody else when
she got home, but not him. It had been a particularly frustrating
and demoralizing day at work. Then the commute home had been
brutal. The drycleaners had lost her favorite sweater. And the
squirrels had cleaned out all the birdfeeders. She was exhausted,
angry, irritable, and one aggravation away from tears. She had
been looking forward to some quiet time with Milton, where she
could get some sympathy and support. When she came back
from the phone call to find that he was tucked away in his study,
THEN she was angry with him.

When they got into bed that night, Charlene turned away from Milton and didn't acknowledge his "Good night." Milton at that point felt confirmed in his belief that she had been mad at him earlier and convinced that the greatest safety would be found in keeping his distance from her. The angrier she got, the more distance he sought. The more distance he kept, the angrier she became. And so it continued. When Charlene brought it up, finally, she spoke so angrily about Milton's withdrawal that he retreated even farther in order to protect himself from her rage.

In an ironic twist, Charlene, wanting distance from her pain at Milton's detachment, eventually told Milton that she wanted a separation. Just as ironically, that provoked Milton to put aside his distancing defense and approach Charlene with a statement of his love for her and his commitment to the marriage.

Once they were willing, if only out of desperation, to talk things through, the subject arose of how Milton would "hide out" when Charlene was angry and prickly. Charlene grabbed the opportunity to try to explain to Milton what was really going on for her at those times.

"Milton, it's rarely about you. I deal with the world all day and I come home to you as a sanctuary. Those times when it's not about you are the times when I particularly need you. I feel thoroughly rejected and abandoned when you go away at those times."

"Charlene, it's scary to be around you then, 'cause I'm afraid that you're going to let loose with everything I'm doing wrong and be really angry with me, especially about stuff I don't know how to fix."

As they talked, they came up with what they hoped would be a solution. Charlene said that she'd try to let Milton know directly at those times that it wasn't about him, so that he'd know that it was both safe and necessary for him to stick around. Milton said that he'd to try too to ask her at those times if it was about him; but that it was way scary to do that, since then he'd be in the line of fire if it <u>was</u> about him. He thought that inviting such a potentially contentious exchange might be beyond his current capacity. But he did feel confident that he could stick around when she was prickly as long as he knew that he wasn't the one she was so upset with. He really wanted to be there for her when she needed him, so this let him do that without feeling at risk.

This solution allowed Milton to approach Charlene instead of seeking safety in distance. And Charlene didn't have to pursue Milton to get what she needed from him. Milton felt much more successful as a partner; and Charlene felt much safer in her relationship with Milton. The perfect win-win.

Although it may not always seem so, the most productive course in these situations is to *ask* if you want to find out if your partner's negative feelings are about you. The very act of asking is an affirmation of commitment and caring. The asking itself is likely to reduce any anger that may in fact be directed toward you.

If you recognize that you're giving off an angry aura that your partner may not be able accurately to interpret, it's a good idea to reassure your partner that it's not about him or her. This clears the way for your partner to approach rather than avoid.

As is so often the rule, don't assume that you know what your partner is thinking; don't assume that your partner knows what you're thinking.

♥

Wrong is assuming that your partner is assuming
whatever you're assuming.

♥

It's what you're used to

Which of the following are "right"?
Women cook and men clean the pots and pans.
Men grill and women do the prep work.
Presents get opened Christmas morning.
One present gets opened Christmas Eve.
All Chanukah presents get opened the night of the first candle.
Women do not work outside the home.
Men vacuum and women dust.
Men scrub bathtubs and toilets.
Men mow and women trim hedges.
The cook never cleans.

Chances are that you nodded in agreement to some of the above and made a "that's ridiculous!" face to some of the others. Of course, it was a trick question. There is no universal right or wrong in these particular situations. But, depending on what you grew up with, you were likely to find some of these arrangements more or less acceptable. In fact, depending on what you were used to in your home when you were growing up, you were likely to find some of the statements above either self-evident or appalling.

The key of course is that, since partners come from different homes, they may find different things self-evident and appalling. Some of those differences are easily resolved. You may prefer the way something was done in your partner's family, so it may be a welcome opportunity to make a change. Or your partner may care a lot about something about which you care very little. For example, your partner may consider church attendance every

Sunday to be tremendously important, while you were raised in a non-attending family. It may be something about which you are enthusiastic despite its divergence from your family's traditions. Or maybe you are fine with it since it matters so much to your partner but wouldn't attend on your own. Not every deviation from your origins will present a problem. But, inevitably, some will.

It's not really practical to rule out every potential partner who may have different experiences and expectations, since that would rule out everybody. The objective becomes to address divergent expectations and find ways to deal with them.

Some of those expectations need to be addressed very early in a relationship. For example, a woman committed to career development has no future with a man who believes that women should not work outside the home. A man counting on a two-income household has no future with a woman who intends to be a fulltime stay-at-home mom.

But most of the divergences that crop up can be handled from within a relationship. It is usually possible to resolve issues and differing expectations to the reasonable satisfaction of both parties. It is most possible, however, when these differences are addressed BEFORE they wreak havoc. Talking about when to open presents is best addressed, for example, before Christmas Eve or the first night of Chanukah. Who cooks or who cooks where, who cleans or who cleans what are questions that you should assume that you need to address. Assuming that your partner has exactly the same expectations that you do can result in some very disappointed, angry, or surprised partners.

If you grew up in a household in which your dad did the laundry, you could be unpleasantly surprised to run out of underwear when your husband doesn't spontaneously do the laundry that you've been heedlessly throwing into the hamper. If you grew up in a household in which your mom mowed the lawn, you could be puzzled as to why the grass keeps getting higher and your wife never seems to pull out the lawnmower. Shouldn't someone be cleaning those toilets? Wasn't your partner going to be balancing the checkbook?

There is no one right answer to who does what. The one wrong answer is assuming that your partner is assuming whatever you're assuming.

♥

The problem is reframed as one of data
collection and information sharing.

♥

When water runs uphill, go with the flow

"She's being totally illogical."
"How could such a smart man be so stupid?!"

When your partner does or says something that appears completely illogical or senseless, what do you do with that? A likely response is to reject the behavior in some way. We say, "She couldn't mean that," or, "That's ridiculous." But these responses are not particularly helpful in moving the conversation forward. In fact, they make things grind to an angry, frustrated halt.

Mike was an aeronautical engineer. He was a bright, accomplished man who spent his professional time making things work. He derived great satisfaction from observing the highly predictable behavior of his machines. When something didn't behave in the expected fashion, he was, despite his disappointment, always eager to solve the puzzle of why it had behaved in an unanticipated way.

When Mike came in to therapy with Jean, a biologist, she was very angry with Mike and thoroughly frustrated. She couldn't understand why a man of Mike's obvious intelligence was so stupid with her. She was intelligent and articulate – why did all their personal conversations end up basically with her saying, "You just refuse to understand!", and him saying, "That's because you make no sense!"?

Since Mike had obvious talent for problem-solving at work, our first goal was to apply those same gifts at home. I asked him what he did at work if, say, a wing design didn't perform as he expected. Did he throw up his hands in disgust and declare the results impossible? He told me that that was when he had to figure out how to modify his model to include this new bit of data. I asked, "What if you found water to run uphill?" Continuing the thinking, he said, "Well, then you figure out what the rules are that make this happen." Bingo!

When Mike was in his scientist mode, he knew absolutely that data <u>had</u> to make sense. It was just a question of figuring out the rules, even if they were different from what he expected. This same principle applies to people. Requiring your partner to fit your expectations instead of expanding your understanding to fit your partner's behavior is like Mike requiring his wing design to fit the formula instead of changing the formula to fit the data. If something's happening right before your eyes, it's supremely illogical to declare that it shouldn't.

Both men and women tend to do this with their partners. We all function from some model of understanding the world. But any two people have two different models from which to work. And the models for male and female people can be very different. Requiring your partner to function within the rules of <u>your</u> model is unrealistic. To declare their behavior "wrong" or "senseless" when it doesn't match your expectations is highly illogical as well as disrespectful. Just like Mike's airplane designs, if the data doesn't match the model, the model must change or the wing will never work the way you need it to. In truth, it's much less painful and much more productive to change a model than it is to try to defend an inaccurate model against the facts. Whatever satisfaction may lie in maintaining the rightness of your thinking is pretty small compared to the satisfaction of two people whose thinking evolves to give them increased understanding and closeness.

Once Mike had realized for himself that rejecting data was counterproductive, he was quick to figure out that the obvious solution was to collect more data. The more information he had from which to work, the more confident he could be that he could learn to understand and predict this world. So he asked Jean questions and listened carefully to the answers.

For Jean's part, she was surprised to discover that what she thought was intuitively obvious was not in fact at all obvious to Mike. Expecting him to understand automatically what was obvious to her was just as illogical as his approach had been. She had to recognize that he too was working from a different model. It was her responsibility to provide data, even when that meant explaining something that she thought he "should" understand. It was in her best interest for him to understand more about her experience, so it was her job to share more data in a respectful way.

She couldn't expect him to fit her expectations either. Her model also had to expand to include his different way of seeing things if she was to be successful in understanding and predicting his behavior and meeting his needs. So, she too needed to set about collecting data from him. He also then had to provide it in a respectful fashion, without expecting that it was as obvious to her as it was to him.

Once the problem was reframed as one of data collection and information sharing, both parties were able to be open and eager to receiving and transmitting their respective experiences. Inquiry trumped expectation; data trumped assumption. Understanding followed.

As the data comes together in increasingly coherent fashion, models (or maps) will evolve that both partners will find useful. Both partners end up feeling more successful and more secure, more understood and less frustrated.

♥

A failure to intuit or a failure to observe
is NOT the same as a failure to love.

♥

Getting from where you are to where you want to be

*T*he myth says that when you love someone you just know intuitively what they feel, want, and need. It says that if someone loves you, they'll know. The dark side of the myth is the conclusion, therefore, that if your partner doesn't know intuitively, then he or she doesn't love you. This is not only not true, it's damaging because it leads people to misinterpret a partner's behavior and motivation.

It's true that some people are highly intuitive. It's also true that an observant partner can ascertain all sorts of information over time. It is NOT true that a failure to intuit or a failure to observe is the same as a failure to love.

It IS true that a partner who makes an effort to know is felt to be a loving partner.

While observation can be very valuable, nothing is as foolproof as asking your partner and listening closely to the answer. Your partner wants to be understood. By understanding your partner, you become more able to behave in ways that are both successful and gratifying for both of you.

When an honest and open exchange occurs between partners, they take another step toward creating a map of their relationship. It becomes possible and likely that partners will move beyond old assumptions and old experiences and create a new understanding based on the here and now. As with all maps, it makes it easier to get from where you are to where you want to be.

♥

It isn't necessary for both partners to see things the same way.
It's only necessary to understand how your partner sees it.

♥

Relationship maps

*L*inda was in tears, but she was also furious with Stu. "How can you ask me to do that?! Don't you understand me at all, even after 10 years?"

Stu was confused and felt guilty about Linda's distress, but he was at a loss about what he might have said that was so upsetting to Linda. His impulse was to defend what he'd just said as perfectly reasonable and to question the logic of her response. But he'd been down that path before – it led nowhere good. She'd be offended that he considered her unreasonable and only more convinced that he was insensitive. He was determined to have a better outcome this time. Since he was clueless about the nature of her feelings, he decided that the logical step was to ask her to explain them to him. He always felt better when he had more information with which to work. He was anxious though that she might consider his ignorance an indication of indifference.

To his amazement, instead of being angry with him for being clueless, she instead stopped crying and looked like she'd been given a gift. She started tentatively, a few words at a time, looking at him to see if he were really listening. He remained attentive, and then he asked some questions to clarify what she meant by certain words. It was as if some magic were occurring between them. When he said, "Now I understand," it was for her as if a rainbow had suddenly bloomed around them.

So what happened between Linda and Stu? For all of us, it's natural to believe that our sense of reality is our partner's sense of reality. If I look at the wall and see that it's pretty and green, I expect you to look at the wall and see it the same way. But two separate people always have two different perceptions of reality. We each bring different history to the relationship, different experience, which causes us to see things from our unique personal perspective. Even green walls look different depending on whether you were <u>forced</u> or <u>permitted</u> to paint your childhood bedroom walls green.

When Stu asked Linda what her experience was, he was acknowledging that her perception might be different from his. He was demonstrating that he had a commitment to understanding her experience. And he took a very constructive step – he gathered information on her perception so that he could build in his own mind a picture of *her* reality. Once he'd made this picture he understood what had happened between them that caused a fight. He also had the beginnings of a map that would help him navigate her experience in the future.

For example, if I look at the floor between us and see carpet, I expect you to see carpet also. But what if when you look, you see not carpet but an endlessly deep gorge? If I don't know what it is that you see, then I don't understand (and consider it irrational) when you refuse to walk across that floor to my side of the room. But, since you see a deadly gorge, you consider it very insensitive of me to ask you to cross the floor.

It isn't necessary for both partners to see the floor the same way. It's only necessary to understand how your partner sees it. When both partners understand the gorges that exist in each other's reality, then they can build relationship maps that allow them to navigate with understanding and sensitivity.

The only way to build the map is by exploring the territory. And the way to do this is to share your experience with your partner and to solicit your partner's experience. The information that you gather through asking and telling helps you both to build a relationship map.

For Linda and Stu, the fight turned into a valuable opportunity to share experience. Stu learned why Linda was so upset. Not only was he able to make her feel better, but he was able to avoid repeating the same frustrating pattern over and over again.

Linda came to understand that Stu wasn't being willfully unkind but was perceiving things differently. She came to appreciate that his intentions had in fact been loving. As he came to understand her experience better, he was able to translate those loving intentions more successfully into words and actions that she could understand and appreciate.

Relationships are easier with a map, one you create for yourselves through an exchange of information. When that exchange comes from a place of truly wanting to understand, the exchange itself feels loving and validating.

♥

Partners can work together to put away the past
in service of the future.

♥

Archiving old wounds

*O*ne of the hardest things to do with a computer is to get it to forget something that was saved. Once it's saved to the hard disk, information is very tenacious. Even when you delete something, it turns out that mostly what you're doing is just deleting the name of the file. It's like trying to get the computer to forget that it still has the information. The information remains on the hard drive. This is why there are professionals and businesses that can make a career out of reconstructing "lost" data.

In a relationship, events are also stored in memory. As many a rueful spouse has discovered, once stored this memory is very hard to clear. Instead of trying to "delete" a memory, which is next to impossible, it makes more sense instead to try to *archive* a memory.

When you archive something, you put it away. It is typically placed somewhere that is accessible but well out of the way. The intention is to retain the ability to retrieve it if you need it, but to keep it from intruding on your current "desktop," or in your life, and using up valuable space, time, and energy.

In a troubled relationship, it is common to find the relationship space very cluttered with old items – old fights, old wounds, old resentments. Even the oldest issues may never have been resolved and put to rest. What happened today and what happened 10 years ago are both being fought about as if they are equally current and equally important. It can be very discouraging to try to work on moving a relationship forward when you have to tread through the debris of every fight or wound that has not been resolved or put aside.

Sometimes one partner tries to clear out the space by demanding that the other partner, "just forgive and forget already!"

Practically speaking, a partner is unlikely to be able or willing to do this. But, under certain circumstances, a partner may be both able and willing to archive one or more old issues.

For example, Bill and Daria had been married for 13 years. Over the years they had had many fights. In most of those fights, Daria had brought up the time, in their first year of marriage, when Bill had gone out after work with his coworkers and, without a word to her, not come home 'til the wee hours. She'd been worried sick at the time. Since then she'd just been angry. Now every time he behaved in a way that appeared to her to be particularly inconsiderate of her feelings she brought up the original insult.

Bill honestly regretted having worried her so badly in the first place. He never meant to hurt her or cause her worry. Every time he did he felt sorry and guilty. But he was also feeling resentful that this almost-13 year old incident was being used to beat on him. He'd tried apologizing; but even if she accepted his apology, she'd resurrect the whole thing for the next fight. He wondered if she'd ever let it go.

Daria was so frustrated. No matter how many times she'd told Bill how his inconsiderate behavior upset her, he'd repeat the behavior. Oh, it would take a different form each time. But from her point of view, it was all the same. That's why it all seemed to have been presaged by that incident in their first year of marriage.

Bill wanted Daria to delete the memory. Daria couldn't do that. From her point of view, not only had it been singularly painful at the time, but it was still relevant to what was happening now.

She was willing however to consider archiving the memory.

If Bill would be able and willing to articulate that he understood her feelings and demonstrate that he was working to be considerate of her feelings, then she'd promise not to bring up the early incident, no matter how provoked or justified she felt. She'd commit to address only what was happening now.

This way they'd both get what they really wanted. Bill would finally be free of the futile effort to erase an early failing and would no longer feel damned to carry it on his shoulders for all eternity. Daria would get the validation and responsiveness that she'd been craving for years. They'd both get the feeling that the marriage was moving forward unencumbered by the past. And they'd feel that it was happening because of their collaborative efforts and mutual commitment to the marriage.

Forgetting may not be possible. Moving forward without perpetually carrying past mistakes may be entirely possible, IF partners work together to put away the past in service of the future

♥

If behavior changes <u>now</u> because of something understood
about the past,
a partner can feel safe in putting away the past.

♥

A clean slate

*J*ane and Adam were in unfortunately familiar territory in this fight. Mostly they got along okay; but then something relatively small would happen and it would set off a bigger fight.

This time it was the trash. Adam couldn't believe that he was standing in his living room having a screaming fight with Jane about the trash.

"Jane, it's just trash, for heaven's sake. Calm down."

"Do <u>not</u> tell me to calm down, Adam. And it's not 'just' trash. This is just one more example of me not being able to count on you."

"Jane, get real. I forgot to take the trash down. It's not the end of the world."

"Adam, that is so like you. Always minimizing, minimizing all the things you've screwed up in our marriage."

"What are you talking about? You make it sound like I've been some horrible person for 20 years."

"Wouldn't you call it horrible when a man disappears on a two day bender and is AWOL for your mother's funeral?" she hissed at him.

"For crying out loud, Jane, your mom died 15 years ago. Let it go. I made a mistake. I'm sorry. Can't I move on with a clean slate?"

"No, you cannot. How am I supposed to do that? How do I forget something that painful and upsetting? Well, I can't. I remember it."

"Well, how come you don't remember just as well all the times I <u>didn't</u> let you down? Huh, Jane, how come?" He was sounding belligerent, he knew, but he was feeling unfairly judged. After all, most of the time he was a reasonably decent husband, he thought. In his opinion, he should be judged on the majority of his behavior, not the exceptions. The exceptions shouldn't stay on his "record".

Jane took a long, slow breath. "Okay, Adam, let me try to explain this in another way." She wasn't yelling anymore; she was working hard at speaking calmly. She really wanted him to understand finally what this was about for her, and why his wish for a "clean slate" was beyond her means to grant. "Remember when you tore your ACL when you fell into that hole outside the restaurant, where the construction was going on and the orange cone had been stolen?"

"Of course I remember that. It was a nightmare. It hurt so badly and I was so scared about needing surgery. I remember every detail of that evening from the moment that I hit that stupid hole."

"That was 16 years ago, you know. And you remember every detail. And you still won't go back to that restaurant. So why don't you 'let it go'? And do you remember every detail of every evening since then? You know, all the evenings that you didn't fall into a hole. Of course not. What you remember so vividly, with so much pain that you still wince when you think about it, is the night that you got hurt."

Adam sat down and remained quiet. He realized that he was unconsciously rubbing his knee. It was true. Thinking about that night brought it all back. It really didn't feel 16 years ago; it felt pretty close. And it was true – he had been unwilling ever to return to that stupid restaurant, even though they had apologized profusely and offered him a free meal for himself and a guest. He always said that he just didn't trust them. He'd heard from quite a few friends that they'd had lovely meals there. And nobody else had gotten hurt. Still, the place had such a horrible association for him that he just wouldn't go there.

He stared at his knee for a long time, frowning as he considered what she'd said. Then he looked up at Jane with the beginning of a new understanding. "I think I get it. You can't just forget and let it go because you were hurt, badly hurt. You need to feel that you aren't setting yourself up to get hurt again the same way if you let it go. You're looking to *me* to prove to *you* that it's safe to move past the bad memories." He paused, thinking about all of this. "I think I finally understand something—when I do something that reminds you of that hurt, even something that I think is a small thing, it makes you think that nothing has changed, that I don't care."

She looked at him wide-eyed and said nothing. She was a little scared to say anything for fear of breaking the spell.

He continued. "I hurt you and made the bad memory for you. It's my responsibility to help you feel that it's different now. It's not your responsibility to forget the event." He frowned as he considered that. Then he looked up at her.

"Can I ever get that clean slate that I wanted?" he asked. "Is that possible?"

"Adam, I honestly don't know. But I think maybe the slate could fade over time 'til it could get hard to read." Jane's voice and posture had changed. She sounded hopeful now instead of angry and she was no longer standing so rigidly.

As long as Jane felt that nothing had changed, she needed to hold onto the past for her own protection. BUT—

If Adam can demonstrate that his behavior changes because of something he now understands, then Jane can feel safer about putting away the past.

If Adam understands now why his reliability is such a hot button for Jane, then Jane doesn't have to keep bludgeoning him with the past in order to get him to pay attention to her feelings.

If Jane experiences Adam as responsive to her needs and feelings, she can begin to see him as reliable and trustworthy.

THEN she can begin to trust that he now understands the past and will work to make the future different.

♥

With greater understanding comes
greater relationship success and satisfaction.

♥

Innocent or hurtful? Maybe both

We are, naturally, more aware of our own intentions than we are of the likely impact of our actions on another person. We can sometimes act out of innocent intentions and still hurt someone we care about, albeit unintentionally. It is incumbent upon us to make every effort to understand our partners in an attempt to avoid inflicting such hurt. It is not legitimate simply to say always, "I didn't know."

That's not to say that there isn't honest ignorance. But part of the commitment to a partner involves the sincere intention to come to understand *more*. Of course there will be incidents in which you unintentionally offend. The key however is whether you utilize such events as opportunities in which to learn more about your partner so as to understand him or her better. The hope and expectation is that greater understanding leads to fewer of those unintended woundings.

When there is evidence of a learning curve (that is, a change in behavior as a result of experience), it is persuasive that there is a commitment to understanding and change. In the absence of a learning curve, there is the sense of a partner's indifference. A failure to grow in understanding will be experienced as a willful disregard of a partner's feelings. Feeling disregarded will lead to disappointment, resentment, hurt, and hopelessness.

On the other hand, when your partner's behavior changes because of some new understanding of you, you experience instead affirmation, validation, and a sense of connectedness.

If you demonstrate a wish to understand, and if that understanding influences your behavior, then your partner experiences you as committed to the relationship.

With greater understanding comes greater relationship success and satisfaction, for both partners.

♥

Looking at other women was like shopping around,
which implied dissatisfaction with his wife.

♥

Looking for trouble

Scott shot a lingering look at the woman in the low-cut dress. He recalled that he was with his wife and shifted his attention to Amy. She looked beautiful tonight. Scott smiled with pleasure at his wife of 14 years and was stunned to receive a glare in return.

It took him a moment to realize why she was angry and then dismissed it with a blush and, "C'mon, Amy. It was nothing. Let's enjoy the evening."

Scott kept up a light patter as the meal progressed, hoping that the passage of time and the intervention of a good meal would mellow Amy's mood. Scott watched Amy get angrier instead. Realizing that avoiding the subject was not working, Scott decided to approach it directly.

Scott smiled apologetically, reaching to take her hand, and said, "I'm sorry. It's no big deal. Let's just put this whole thing behind us."

Amy pulled her hand away and said, coldly, "I'm ready to leave."

Having his apology rejected made Scott hurt and confused."Look, Amy, it was no big deal. I only looked at her for a second."

"Did you enjoy the look, Scott?," Amy asked acidly.

Scott was at a loss here. Of course he'd enjoyed the look. So what? But he was reasonably certain that if he said so, he'd be in worse trouble. He decided to try an apology again.

"I'm sorry. I never meant to upset you. Can't we just move on now?"

Amy said, "Never mind. Let's just go home."

As she seemed to be willing to let it go, Scott felt relieved and dropped the subject.

Even though Amy didn't mention the restaurant incident again, she seemed to be generally short-tempered with him for the next several days. Finally, she blew up at him for something that had nothing to do with him. That's when Scott called a marriage counselor.

Amy described what she'd felt when Scott looked at the blonde outside the restaurant.

"I felt like the ugly stepsister. She was in her early twenties and drop-dead gorgeous. I'm not. What's to keep him from dropping me like a hot potato and having a merry old time with her? Or with the next younger or prettier woman he meets?"

Scott's defense was to dismiss this as nonsense. He'd never been one to run around. From his point of view, he'd never given her any reason at all to doubt his fidelity. Amy rather angrily pointed out that he looked at other women. For Scott, the two things were unrelated and he was at a loss to follow the connection.

As they continued to explore Amy's experience, Scott figured out that, from Amy's point of view, looking was like shopping around. In Amy's mind, for Scott to look implied a lack of satisfaction with Amy. Since he'd simply thought of looking as a normal male reflex, with absolutely no greater meaning, he was stunned to recognize the powerful messages that it carried for her.

Amy was asked to tell Scott directly what it was that she needed to hear from him in order to feel less troubled by such incidents. She had to be persuaded that it wasn't obvious to him already. And only Scott could persuade her that he really wanted to know.

She took a stab at it. "I want to hear that he's satisfied with me and with our marriage. Maybe not perfectly, but enough. I want to hear that he loves me now as much as he did when we got married. I need to hear that he finds me attractive. I need to hear that he'll still love me 15 years from now, when I'm even less young and less attractive."

Scott protested, "But all those things are true! You know that, Amy."

He had to be persuaded that she really didn't know and that the only way she would know it was to hear it from him.

He came to understand that Amy needed to hear these things straight out and hear them regularly, particularly at moments when her anxiety was triggered. Since these things were true and he really wanted her to feel secure within their marriage, it wasn't particularly difficult for Scott. Even when his eyes were magnetically attracted to a bombshell, he could turn the moment into a net gain between them by anticipating and acting on Amy's need for reassurance. When a beautiful, younger woman walked by, Amy got a hug and a statement of commitment. He told her how beautiful she was and how much he loved her.

Scott's constancy in his sensitivity to these moments reassured Amy in a way that lame and dismissive apologies never could.

Even though he'd had neither expectation of nor intention to hurt her with his "innocent" looking, he learned that it *was* hurtful. And, most importantly, he changed his behavior as a result of what he'd learned. His sensitivity to her feelings was a powerful persuasion of his commitment to her.

♥

Issues can be of such fundamental importance
that people react to them strongly, viscerally,
and often at the speed of a reflex.

♥

Meta issues

*D*ifferent people have different sensitivities, different things to which they react particularly strongly. Men and women in particular often have different sensitivities. It is not uncommon, for example, to have women feel more sensitive to feelings of disconnection, while men are likely to feel more sensitive to issues of autonomy. These issues are of such fundamental importance that people react to them strongly, viscerally, and often at the speed of a reflex. These sensitivities can be born not only of gender but also of personal experience, cultural norm, family exposure, or perhaps even genetic makeup. By the time someone is in a relationship, it may be difficult or impossible to assign origin to any given sensitivity.

It is easy to recognize such a sensitivity in action. If for example you see someone intentionally do exactly the opposite of what he was told to do, you may be observing such a sensitivity. The oppositional behavior may have had little if anything to do with what he was told to do. It was instead a response to the nature of the communication. It didn't matter what he was told to do, only that he was told to do something. In this case the sensitivity may be to a communication that appears to assume authority (someone else's) and deny autonomy (his). By doing the opposite of what he was told to do, the recipient of the communication may be demonstrating that he IS autonomous and will not accede to the transmitter's authority. He has "proven" his autonomy by not behaving in a compliant way. His autonomy survives this perceived challenge from the other person.

The partner on the other hand may have been unaware of how this communication was received. She may have had only the intention to be efficient in trying to accomplish a particular task. When her partner did not comply with her instruction, her sensitivity may have been triggered in turn. She may have perceived his noncompliance as a willful refusal to meet her needs. At that point her sensitivity to feelings of emotional abandonment may have been provoked. She may become more assertive in her instructions to him in an effort to get him to demonstrate that he remains connected to her and that therefore he wants to be responsive to her emotional needs.

As she pushes harder in hopes of achieving a reassuring response from him, he pulls away more aggressively in an attempt to assert his independence. Each person becomes more mobilized to meet his or her own needs, thereby provoking exactly the feared response from the partner.

At no point was the actual content of the tasks involved relevant to the behavior observed. All choices were instead dictated by the overarching emotional needs and sensitivities of the people involved. These overarching needs and sensitivities are the "meta" issues. "Meta" in this use simply means "beyond"—beyond the obvious content of the communication, into issues more powerful and more mobilizing.

Not all "meta" issues are universal. Not all men react one way or women another. What matters in constructing a successful relationship is understanding what your "meta" issues are and what your partner's "meta" issues are. They are there; they are going to affect your communication and your relationship. Your understanding of the "meta" issues gives you power to see them and to address them, instead of being the unwitting victim of them.

If you have come to understand that your partner is very sensitive to any communication that he perceives as a command, then you can modify your communication behavior to avoid command-sounding language. For example, "bring the ladder" feels like a command. But "I'd like to clear off that top shelf; can you please bring the ladder?" sounds like a respectful request.

Similarly, responding to the above communication with a flat "no" feels emotionally disconnected. Responding instead with, "Hands are full; be there in a sec." feels responsive.

The Meta issues are always there, awaiting some trigger. They always have the potential to influence whether the interpersonal event is experienced as positive or negative. The more you listen and understand, the better prepared you are to be successful, avoiding minefields that might otherwise be treacherous territory.

♥

If the same argument takes place over and over,
it suggests that something else is going on.

♥

What I said wasn't what I was talking about

"I've asked him a thousand times to put the car keys on the hook. He just doesn't bother."

"I left them in a perfectly reasonable place, but it has to be her way all the time."

Mark and Beth were both frustrated, hurt, and angry. They both insisted that what they were arguing about was obvious – the keys. They both felt that they'd been perfectly clear and coherent, repeatedly. Why was the other person being so difficult?!

I suggested that perhaps the message (where to put the keys) was only part, and not the most important part, of their communication. If the same argument takes place over and over again without satisfaction, it suggests that something else is going on, perhaps beyond awareness. It's at this other level that important issues are not being openly addressed. This is the "meta" level – a level over and above the obvious level of conversation. The message level of their conversation had to do with keys. But what about the "meta" level?

When I asked about <u>feelings</u> around their communications, we tapped into the "meta" level. He described feeling criticized for every little thing he did. He felt that she wanted to run things her way and he was under orders all the time. She found this mystifying. There had been no intention to criticize or to command. She thought she'd explained quite logically why the keys needed to be on the hook – if they weren't there, she worried that she wouldn't be able to find them in time to get to work on schedule. Her mornings were stressful enough without one more bit of aggravation.

She saw no sense to his feelings. In fact, she felt very hurt that he apparently didn't care at all about her needs, even when she'd explained them repeatedly. She felt emotionally abandoned by his apparent unresponsiveness. He was equally mystified – what did keys have to do with whether he loved her?

The answers for both of them were to be found in the differing nature of communication for men and women. Psycholinguists have described that within men's communication there's always the issue of hierarchy – who's one-up, who's one-down? Who's in charge and who's subordinate? Within women's communication is always the issue of connection – is the connection intact and active (which produces comfort and security)? Or is there a lack of connection (which produces discomfort and insecurity)?

For Mark, the way in which Beth communicated her need felt like a command, implying that she was in charge and he was subordinate. Her commentary on what he was doing and her explanations felt like the kind of criticism and education a parent might deliver to a child. This was an implicit challenge to his sense of his own identity as a man. If he was subordinate or a child, then he was inadequate and therefore incapable of fulfilling his job as a man and a husband. To refuse to accept this definition of himself was a matter of self-respect. So he fought back – he repeatedly refused to do what she asked.

For Beth, Mark's persistent refusal to act in accordance with her requests registered as a disregard for her needs. She felt that her explanations should have communicated that she had a need. Since her message level had been clear and repeated, his behavior had to be coming not from a failure of understanding but from an absence of caring. For her this was repeated evidence of a failure of connection. If he didn't care enough to meet this small need, how could she trust him to meet the big ones? She was hurt and scared. So she gave him another opportunity to demonstrate that he loved her – she explained it again, perhaps in even more basic terms, just to ensure that he understood.

As long as they stayed at the message level they could continue this same unsuccessful conversation indefinitely, in angrier and angrier terms, without coming to a resolution.

The alternative was to address the issues that existed on a "meta" level – her need to feel secure in their connection and his need to feel that she respected him as nothing less than an equal partner. Since Mark was thoroughly committed to Beth and Beth respected Mark deeply, these issues, once identified, were able to be addressed directly and resolved. Then it was possible to develop new ways of communicating on the message level that recognized their needs for respect and responsiveness.

It's by understanding your partner's emotional terrain that you learn how and where to build the bridges that'll carry you forward together.

♥

Integrating the wish to be connected
with the wish for autonomy.

♥

You + I = We, sort of

*T*odd and Cindy were still basking in the glow of the birth of their son when they started to feel an unfamiliar friction between them. They were at a loss to understand why the happiest event of their lives was being followed by increasing irritability toward each other. They were picking fights over the stupidest things, each increasingly unhappy with the other.

The '60s virtually made a religion of finding oneself, but a primary life-task for any person is to develop and clarify a sense of individual identity. This process meets a major challenge when romantic connections enter the picture. How do you integrate the wish to be connected with the wish for autonomy? The desire for intimacy with the desire to be separate? The need to be connected with the need to be independent? These conflicting desires exist in both men and women. But for men and women, the ideal balance may be very different.

Once an intimate relationship is established and stable, many men are likely to invest energy in protecting their independence. They're more likely to see the danger in intimacy as one of compromising their separateness. At the same time, many women are more likely to invest their energy in promoting connectedness. The risk is perceived to lie in being emotionally dis-connected. Over time partners tend to find their comfortable balance between independence and connection. Anything that happens to disturb the balance in a relationship can launch the partners in opposing directions in an effort to re-establish that balance in a form that feels safe and gratifying.

The birth of a new baby, for instance, can be a joyous and welcome event in a couple's life, yet it may also trigger a cascade of relationship consequences. A common scenario is this: Mom is, appropriately, focused on care of the newborn. She takes pleasure and reassurance from her husband's participation in infant care in part because it represents to her that he's connected with her by being engaged where she's engaged.

Any lack of participation is interpreted as a dis-connection from her, a rupture in affiliation. Mom's sense of equilibrium has been disturbed by the change of status from wife to wife-and-mother. Now more than ever she needs to feel that her connection with her husband is secure enough to withstand life's challenges. So Mom wants Dad to participate more.

By becoming a parent, Dad has just undertaken the biggest sacrifice of independence of his life. For the rest of his days he's bound to and responsible for this child. (While this is true for Mom also, it generally has a different emotional impact on men and women.) It not uncommonly occurs that this massive loss of independence for a man (however voluntary) is followed directly by a powerful need to re-establish a sense of independence, to assert that he may have given up this piece of his separateness, but he still maintains his ownership of the remainder. He feels a need to preserve his identity as separate-from-wife-and-child. So, when Mom asks Dad to join her in childcare, his reflexive response may be a hearty, "no".

The obvious content of the communications is about participation in childcare. The "meta" issues are of connection and independence.

His declaration of independence bumps directly into her quest for connection. The more she attempts to solicit his participation as a sign of connection, the more he feels his independence is being challenged. He defends it more and more aggressively, which she perceives as a potent threat to their affiliation.

This can become a self-perpetuating downward spiral, each move of one partner triggering the complementary move that leads to the inevitable response. If the underlying needs (independence and affiliation) are not identified and understood, then each partner may escalate in order to achieve their respective and competing goals. The spiral can, however, be interrupted, and even reversed, if communication at the "meta" level replaces the skirmishes at the content level.

It doesn't take childbirth to shake up a relationship and trigger this dynamic. Anything that has an impact on how time and energy are allotted – a job change, a new friend, an illness – may shift the balance between people. This in turn causes each partner to try to achieve a new balance that reaffirms basic personal needs. If two people are trying to reaffirm different basic personal needs, then the deteriorating spiral described above may occur.

The good news is that this spiral doesn't need to play itself out at length, with each position becoming more entrenched and less accommodating. Affiliation and independence are lifestyle qualities that both partners can relate to, understand, and respect. When good, functional communication occurs between partners – communication that allows for a mutual sharing of experience and a mutual respect for each person's needs – then a balance that's satisfying to both partners can be found and supported. Then there's no need for escalation. Instead, the life change becomes an opportunity to reaffirm commitment to yourself, your partner, and your relationship.

♥

True "success" has to include both family and work.

♥

Men and achievement

*N*athan had been working late every night. The project was finished, finally. When he got home, he practically swaggered into the house. It had been a major triumph professionally and he couldn't wait to share it with Pam. He marched into the bedroom and said, with a flourish of his imaginary sword, "The warrior is home, triumphant!"

Pam, propped up in bed with a book, smiled at his obvious joy and congratulated him, but she seemed subdued. He was puzzled. This was big! If not trumpets, there should at least be hugs and kisses.

"Pam, why aren't you happier? This is great for both of us — respect, prestige, more money."

"Nathan, I feel sort of irrelevant here. Recently you've been away from home so much and you've been consumed with work. You're having a great time with your professional success, but it seems more important to you than I am. What am I — chopped liver?"

"Pam, what are you talking about? Don't you want me to be a success?"

"Of course I want you to be a success. It's just that your interest seems to be directed exclusively toward your job, with little or nothing left for me and the kids."

Nathan leapt to the defensive. "It's not like this project would wait for my convenience. It had to be done now, and I did it. If I hadn't accepted it, someone else would have gotten it. It was a plum, and it's not like it would have waited around 'til I had time."

"You mean like I did?" Pam asked, her voice quiet and her face sad.

Nathan frowned. He was truly at a loss. He loved his wife absolutely and he had no wish to hurt or disappoint her. He was in fact looking forward to more time now to be with her; he loved being with her. But work was work. It had to be done, and done well.

"Nathan, you used to say that I was the most important thing in the world to you."

"You still are, Pam."

"Then why isn't it enough for you to be a successful husband and father? Why is being a big success at work so important?"

Nathan wondered how to explain that, as a man, first he defined himself by his achievement. As a man, no matter how committed he was to his wife and family, his sense of himself was first and foremost determined by his achievements in the world. He was sure that his love for his family was absolute. He would unhesitatingly die for any one of them. How could he explain that this was independent of that?

"Pam, no matter how much I love all of you and you love me, it's not enough to make me feel successful. I need my professional success to complete the picture. I need to feel successful at work and I need other people, especially other men, to recognize my professional achievements. Without that, I wouldn't feel that I was a successful man."

Pam looked hurt, feeling that wife and family were superfluous in his definition of success.

Nathan continued. "Work success wouldn't be enough by itself though. I want to come home to share my success with you. I want to come home to my wife and family and have you be proud of me. I want to present my success to you and have you know that I also do this for you, to make our lives better. Then I feel truly successful."

She didn't totally understood what he was saying, but she was no longer feeling quite as hurt and overlooked. She could hear his sincerity when he talked about wanting to share his success with his family. She really was happy for him, since this meant so much to him, and he meant so much to her. He got his hugs and kisses.

His re-prioritizing of home and family for awhile helped her feel that the scales were a little better balanced again.

Certainly there were more disagreements about how he allotted his time and energy. Pam often wanted more family time. Nathan was often drawn to devote a bigger proportion of his time to his work. The key was talking about it.

Pam understood better now that Nathan needed work success the same way that she needed the warm and loving time with her friends. Both things took them away from the family, he toward achievement, and she toward affiliation.

When Pam felt that she and the kids were being unreasonably neglected, she spoke up, not so much with anger as with a firm reminder to Nathan that true "success" had to include both family and work.

Nathan didn't always understand why his wife and children couldn't just wait until the work demands eased up. But he did recognize that too little attention left the people he most cared about feeling hurt and unimportant. Since he really didn't want that to happen, he tried to be more sensitive to how his focus on his work was being experienced by the people he loved.

It was often a balancing act between work and family. Nathan often felt pulled in both directions. Pam's efforts to understand why he felt as he did made it both more tolerable for her and less painful for him. It was clear that they would never see the world quite the same way. But they both saw the relationship as worth the effort.

♥

Relationships require attention and care in order to remain
vital, vigorous, and resilient.

♥

A relationship is a living organism

Your body – it's there when you need it. But it can't do what you need it to do if you don't take proper care of it. Even the best and strongest body in the world won't function well if it's not given proper nurturance and care. It needs food, water, exercise. If it's not given these things it will wither and weaken and, ultimately, die. Inert objects, like books, or bricks, or buttons, sit there quietly and wait to be needed. They require no active care but are always immediately available to perform their proper function.

Relationships are like your body, not like bricks – living organisms that require attention and care in order to remain vital, vigorous, and resilient. They need to have energy and support, attention and exercise, in order to remain healthy and strong. In the absence of such care, they can become weak, fragile, and incapable of meeting each partner's needs. Relationships are not like bricks— benign neglect cannot be successful. If not nurtured regularly and well, relationships will weaken and will no longer be able to support people and meet their needs. You cannot leave your relationship untended in a corner and expect to come back to it whenever it suits you or you have time or interest to devote to it. What you come back to will be a pale shadow of what you left. All the worthwhile things that you do outside the relationship's boundaries (work, friendships, charitable activities), no matter how important and legitimate, will not take the place of active participation in the care of the relationship itself.

Women are more likely than men to expect to work at and on relationships; they know that relationships have to be nurtured and exercised in order to thrive and survive. Men are more likely to expect relationships to sustain themselves without active attention; they expect them to be stable and sustained without effort.

Although women may more spontaneously address themselves to relationship nurturance, it can't be their responsibility alone to sustain a relationship. One person alone can't keep a relationship healthy and hearty. Being together, talking together, doing things together, sharing hopes and fears and dreams—these are the sorts of things that nurture the living organism that is a relationship.

Don't wait for danger signs before you take care of your relationship. It's always easier to prevent weakness and disease than to treat it. Nurture this organism so that it's there, strong and healthy, when you need it.

Both parties to a relationship must be active participants in providing ongoing sustenance if they want it to live long and prosper.

♥

A positive emotional bank balance
results in a positive attitude towards your partner;
a negative balance contributes to a negative attitude.

♥

The emotional bank account

When you started driving a car you probably received the lecture from one or another parent instructing you on the necessity of keeping your gas tank filled. It was pointed out to you that unless you put gas into the car, you would be getting no driving out of it. It would be, it was pointed out, irrelevant to the car how much you needed to get someplace – no gas, no go.

When you had your first real savings or checking account, you quickly realized on your own that unless you put money into the account, there would be no money to take out of the account. And if you tried to take out more than you had put in, the bank sent you a nasty (and expensive) note informing you that you would get out of the account only what you had put in and not one penny more.

The marital researcher, John Gottman, among others, has used the term "emotional bank account" to refer to this same phenomenon in relationships. The term is useful because it highlights that the "balance" is dynamic, and that there can be either a positive or negative balance. Partners make either "deposits" into or "withdrawals" from the account. Deposits are positive gestures and actions; withdrawals are negative ones. A positive balance results in a positive attitude towards your partner; a negative balance contributes to a negative attitude.

Let's take a simple and common example to explore how this works.

Carina meets John after work at their son's lacrosse game. As Carina walks over to the bleachers, John spots her and waves while smiling broadly, clearly pleased to see her. This is a deposit into the emotional bank account of this couple, creating a credit. Carina sits down next to John and asks if he has "finally" remembered to mail off the insurance papers? John feels chastised for yesterday's failure and his smile fades even as he assures her that it was done first thing this morning. This is a withdrawal from the emotional account. Carina softens and thanks him for taking care of it, thereby making a deposit of her own into the account. She then asks John about his day at work, sympathizes with the stress of breaking in a new secretary, and intermittently touches his hand to communicate support. She's made numerous deposits and the account is nicely "in the black."

Good thing, too, because now Carina gets a call on her cell phone from a coworker informing her that the computer is emitting smoke and all of today's project planning has disappeared. Carina is now going to have to rely on her account credit to soften the blow when she tells John that she'll now be in the office all evening, even though she'd promised to spend the evening with him.

The emotional bank account balance will now strongly influence how much of an impact this turn of events will have on this couple's immediate experience of their relationship. If they've been making adequate deposits into the account, then withdrawals will still result in a positive balance. This means that they'll still feel good about each other and about how they are together. In this case, even though John is disappointed that Carina is leaving him for the evening, he won't be hurt or angry, he won't take it personally, and he won't be resentful.

This is something like when you suddenly have to make a withdrawal from your real bank account, say, for a new hot water heater. You may not be thrilled with having to make the withdrawal and having the expense; but if your positive bank balance is high enough, you'll still feel safe and comfortable even after the withdrawal.

Every couple will, regularly, have to make withdrawals. Life happens and people make mistakes. The positive balance needs to be high enough that there will still be a feeling of safety and comfort afterward. The only way to cover withdrawals is with deposits. Withdrawals can be, as with Carina's computer disaster, unexpected. This makes it all the more important that regular deposits be made in anticipation of unplanned need. This is the famous "saving for a rainy day" philosophy.

Making a deposit into the emotional bank account can be as simple as bringing your partner a cup of coffee in the morning, complimenting a haircut, or stroking a cheek. And what interest you'll accumulate...

♥

The most important weapon in the struggle with gender
differences
is mutual understanding.

♥

Keys to the castle

Nick sounded pretty discouraged when he said, "It really doesn't matter. Nothing I do is enough."

Kris, on the other hand, looked pretty discouraged. "What he does isn't enough because it's nothing. He comes home and does nothing."

"I thought home was a place for relaxing. I work hard all day, not that that counts for anything with you."

"Well, I thought home was a place where people who cared about each other spent time together. But obviously I don't count for anything with you."

Does this fight sound familiar to you? It's classic because it's based on fundamental issues common to most men and women in relationships.

While there's much overlap, men and women tend to approach relationships differently. Once a relationship is established, men are likely to see it as a safe haven where they can retreat and relax away from the demands of the world. For women, the establishment of a relationship is a promise of connection, a safe haven from the unpleasant state of disconnectedness. While there's no obvious conflict between those two goals, in practice they frequently collide.

Men frequently view their female partners as the keeper of the sacred connection flame. Since she's keeping the flame burning, he can feel free to concentrate his energies on those activities that bring him personal, separate satisfaction.

Women, on the other hand, see the flame as something that is continuously created by the active participation of two partners working together. Any failure of participation threatens the continuation of the connection. In fact, any failure of <u>enthusiasm</u> for participation feels very threatening, since it seems to represent a lack of commitment to the connection.

Men are more likely to assume that the connection continues to exist perfectly securely without having to be continuously fussed with. Unless something dramatic happens to endanger the connection directly, they figure it's just the way they left it. In fact, women's efforts to talk about the relationship, or, worse, work on it, are frequently seen by men as dangerous to the relationship. Like a fine watch, it works best if no one goes in and pokes around in it.

Men, like Nick, want to leave demands and efforts outside the doors of the castle. Women, like Kris, find nurturing and comfort from reconnecting with their partners within the walls of the same castle. Nick figures that he's done his bit for the common good by working hard and by coming home. Kris feels that his contribution to the common good requires his active participation in relationship-building once he gets home. His solitary behavior when he gets home feels to her like a slap in the face, a statement that he doesn't care to connect with her. It's not that she doesn't care that he works hard. She respects his commitment to his work. But that commitment appears to her to be unrelated to their relationship.

From Nick's point of view, his commitment to his work contributes to the financial security of their family unit and to the direct comfort of his partner. Furthermore, he comes home after work instead of going out with the guys because he's committed to her and because he enjoys being home with her. Just knowing that she's in the same house brings him a feeling of warm satisfaction.

For Kris, having him in the same house but not being actively engaged with her feels frustrating and disconnected. She wants to be doing things together that actively contribute to the weaving of a fabric of connectedness between them. That he'll put in high amounts of energy at work and not at home feels to her like a statement of low priority for the relationship.

For Nick, having to work at a relationship feels like a contradiction in terms. To him the point of a relationship is not having to work at it. You put in the courtship time, demonstrate permanent commitment (wedding and fidelity), and then you should be able to relax.

For Kris, a relationship is a living thing that requires lots of ongoing investments of time and energy. In return, it promises a feeling of connectedness.

The differences between men and women aren't insurmountable. The most important weapon in the struggle with gender conflicts is mutual understanding. When each partner understands the other's experience, the groundwork is laid for a successful resolution. When loving partners understand each other's experience, the markers exist with which to create a map to a mutually gratifying relationship.

As always, the route to understanding involves successful communication. Once communication has been accomplished, both parties' wishes and needs can be addressed and accommodated. The castle then can be a place where both sanctuary and connection are achieved, albeit not necessarily at the same moment.

♥

Open hands—
a way for two people to come together
lovingly through communication.

♥

Talking with your (open) hands

*W*hat do you see in your mind's eye when you read, "You did that wrong again! You're so insensitive!" You might imagine someone standing and shaking a finger at you in an angry way. I expect that your response might be to withdraw and become defensive, which is a very logical reaction to feeling attacked.

What do you see and feel when you read instead, "I'm frustrated. This is important to me and I need you to understand"? Can you imagine someone reaching toward you with open hands outstretched asking for your help? I imagine that your response might be to approach and be responsive. If there's no attack, there's no need for defense or withdrawal. The impulse is generally to meet a gesture with a matching gesture, whether that gesture is an open expression of need or a hostile act.

Within relationships we're seeking communication – a cooperative venture between two people committed to mutual understanding. True communication is indeed gratifying. It's an opportunity not only to share another person's experience but also to have your own experience heard and understood by another person. There's a sense of connectedness that comes with hearing and being heard.

Sometimes, despite our wishes, what was supposed to be a communion between people becomes instead an adversarial procedure – where two people are committed not to connection but to winning by making sure that the other person loses.

While there's perhaps a satisfaction also to "winning", it's a satisfaction that carries along with it a sense of <u>dis</u>-connectedness. For there to be winners and losers, there must be adversaries instead of allies, people with whom we are at odds instead of people with whom we share a goal. Human beings are social creatures, creatures who seek connectedness. For many people, adversaries are what you settle for when you don't know how to make allies.

In close personal relationships, we're seeking alliance. In fact, the wish for that connectedness is so great that when it's frustrated, the backlash can be furious.

If someone with whom you wish to experience closeness and understanding fails to listen or be responsive, the disappointment is severe because the wish was of such magnitude. The result of that disappointment is pain. As with all pain, the reflex is to defend. And for many people the best defense is a good offense – "Hurt me and I'll hurt you back twice as hard!" So, there you find yourself– hurting and pushing away the one you to whom you most want to be close.

Of course, just as you defended when you were hurt, so will your partner. The cycle deteriorates steadily, each person only trying to protect himself and thereby perpetuating the very sequence that's causing the pain.

It becomes WANT → DISAPPOINTMENT→ PAIN → ANGER → ATTACK.In the short term it feels less painful to attack or withdraw than to try again to achieve connection. In the long term this sequence entrenches disconnection. The more you wanted the connection in the first place the more painful it is when you don't get it.

It's at this point that couples frequently come to therapy, shaking their heads like wounded bears, confused, frightened, and hurt, with no idea of a way out, a way to that connectedness that they so crave.

"Who started it?" As with any circle, it's an exercise in futility to try to find the beginning. Who cares? The point is to stop the cycle, not to assign blame. A better question is, "Who'll stop the cycle by starting a better direction?"

It takes courage to start a new path. Someone has to be the first to approach with open hands, an offering of honest experience and an invitation to your partner to offer their experience. If the open hands carry authentic feeling without offense, the response is likely to match it. If the hands carry instead a disguised attack, that will be perceived and will be met with a matching defensive attack. One of the best ways to ensure that the words don't carry offense is to phrase the message as an "I statement" – "I'm hurt," or "I feel scared," or "I need you to understand." This is approaching with open hands. It states your experience without assigning blame. Conversely, the way to ensure that your message will be met with defensiveness is to phrase the message as a "You statement" – "You're bad", or "You enjoy hurting me," or "All you want is to have fun." These are the angry finger-shaking postures that so predictably elicit defensive attacks. These angry, fault-finding gestures will be met with matching angry gestures.

Using the gestures *literally* can be especially useful if relations have deteriorated to a point where partners are immediately defensive with each other. Approaching a partner with your hands literally open and outstretched as if you are presenting something to be shared can make a potent nonverbal statement about how you're approaching the moment. It tends instantly to set the mood as one of cooperation instead of attack. It can be a useful tool to break a cycle in which the two of you have become trapped.

Open hands meet lovingly. Finger-shaking leads to dis-connection. It's for you to decide. You might say that it's in your hands.

♥

Each of us naturally assumes that our reality is <u>the</u> reality.

♥

Parallax view–
if I'm okay and you're okay, who's right?

*P*arallax – an object appears, falsely, to have moved from one place to another when it's seen from two different locations. Look at an immovable object in front of you (like a tree outside your window). Now close one eye. Now open that eye while closing the other eye. The object presumably didn't jump from one place to another, but it appeared to because your brain received two different impressions of the location of the object. Which one was the "true" location? Since this isn't a Zen meditation exercise, let's just agree that this question doesn't make a whole lot of sense here.

When you use both eyes together, as you normally do, your brain is continually faced with the task of figuring out what to do with two conflicting but apparently equally valid images. When all systems are functioning properly, your brain presents you with a single image that's been synthesized from the two images with which you presented it. That single image is a product of the two images but may be identical to neither one.

Relationships between two people are affected by this same parallax phenomenon. A relationship is inevitably faced with per-spectives even more divergent than two eyes would present. For two separate individuals, like two separate eyes, even identical and simultaneous experiences would be perceived somewhat dif-ferently. But just as with eyes, it's a meaningless exercise to pose the question asking which perception is the "true" one. Each per-ception has validity. The task is to synthesize a perspective that's built from each separate view to construct a way of working that incorporates both, may be identical to neither, but is useful to both people.

The first order of business involves establishing just what the two different perspectives are. Before a synthesis can be accomplished, each person's experience has to be communicated to the other in order that it can be adequately represented in the ultimate relationship-enhancing product.

This is trickier than it sounds. Each of us naturally assumes that our reality is the reality. So the first step is to solicit from our partners a description of *their* reality. This is in itself a very powerful interaction between people. When someone important to you demonstrates a desire to understand your experience and an openness to the possibility that it might be different from their own experience, it sends the message that you matter, the relationship matters, and that there's an awareness of and sensitivity to your separate identity. So even before any attempts at synthesis, both the recognition of parallax and the effort simply to understand it have already enhanced the relationship.

But communicating these individual experiences can be a difficult task, since each of us inevitably works from the expectation that our own experience defines reality – if I look out the window and see that tree, lovely in bloom, I expect that when you look out the window you'll see the same tree, and that you'll see it in the same way. I may not realize that when you look out the window all you see is the grass that needs mowing. That tree, when noticed at all, is the obstacle you must mow around. Which one of us sees the "true" view? Wrong question! A more useful question is, "How do I help my partner understand what I see?"

It's not helpful to ask, "How can I make my partner see it my way?" That's like asking the left eye to see as if it's the right eye. It's not and can't be. But your partner can come to understand how you see things, even sometimes to anticipate how you'll see something. People who care about each other and understand how they each separately experience something can take these divergent perceptions and work with them. They can develop, cooperatively, a way of doing things that appreciates the differences and that may be identical to neither person's individual approach, but which is functional for both people.

The goal isn't for both people to see things identically. The goal is for both people to feel understood and to feel adequately represented in the ultimate outcome. That's when you've gotten to the place where you can say, "I'm okay, you're okay, and we're both right."

♥

He understands male English, and she
understands female English.

♥

If it's an open book test, why are you failing?

*M*aybe you've had some variation of this classic nightmare — you're sitting at a student desk, the teacher hands you the test, she reminds you that it's "open book" and you smile confidently. You open the book and, with horror, realize that the book is written in some strange language which makes no sense to you. Open book indeed! What good is open book when you can't make sense of the book?

Relations between men and women frequently have moments that resemble this nightmare. Like the teacher, each partner believes that the answers are right in front of the other partner. A partner may even give the answers to the test questions and then be thoroughly puzzled and frustrated when the other partner still acts like he or she doesn't have the information. The following is a typical fight:

Sam, recognizing that Meg is upset: "What do you want from me?"

Meg: "I want you to show me that you care about our marriage."

Sam, the next day: Hands her a Hallmark card wishing her a happy anniversary and asks, "What's for dinner?"

Meg: "Keep your stupid card and make your own stupid dinner!"

Sam: "What do you want from me?"

Meg, believing that Sam has the open book, is frustrated. Since Meg believes that Sam has the answers, she assumes that Sam's failure to act in accordance with the answers means that he's disinterested in her requests.

The truth is likely to be substantially more innocent. Just like in the nightmare, giving somebody the answers doesn't help if the answers are in a language that makes no sense to the test-taker. While Sam and Meg both speak and understand English, Sam understands male English, and Meg understands female English. These are languages that are so far apart that even people who are emotionally close may have little capacity to communicate verbally.

Meg thought that telling Sam that she needed demonstrations of his commitment was the open book. He would "read" that message and recognize that he should make dinner reservations at a fancy restaurant, bring her roses, and tell her in his own words that he loved her more now than when he'd proposed. Anyone fluent in female English would be able to read this message easily. Since Meg was unaware that he didn't speak this language, his failure to do what she was asking looked to Meg not like ignorance but indifference.

Sam's male English interpreted her request as one that could be met by an off-the-rack poem and his being there to hand it to her. In his masculine understanding of marriage, being there was the real demonstration that he cared about the marriage. The card was icing, an effort to be sensitive. From his male English point of view, words were cheap. Ninety percent of marriage was showing up, which he unfailingly did. Why couldn't she read that he was demonstrating commitment? What did she want?

Meg looked at his answers and read only that he was a responsible man who enjoyed a married lifestyle. She heard nothing in his male communication that she recognized to mean that he loved <u>her</u>, personally. Showing up was the barest minimum. The stupid blue jays showed up every morning for the peanuts she put out for them. It wasn't a personal attachment to her. She needed something more from Sam.

To each of them, the answers to the test they were giving were to be found in an open book. But the open book they were given might as well have been closed, because it was in a foreign language.

Once you recognize that language is the problem, the answer lies in teaching your language to your partner. Act as if your partner grew up on the moon. Assume nothing beyond your partner's desire to learn. Teach everything from scratch, with all the tolerance you would have for any novice with a commitment to the subject but a background that gets in the way. It's like teaching French to a native German speaker – what background the student has is only going to interfere with the new learning. But lapsing into the wrong language doesn't signify disinterest. Similarly, the power of old habits doesn't excuse a failure to try to learn a new way.

In male-female relationships, both parties need to persist in making efforts both to learn their partner's language and to teach their partner their own language. Becoming bilingual shows tolerance, understanding, and commitment – in other words, love. And it makes conversation much more productive.

♥

A persistent belief that something <u>should</u> work can conquer
experience
that says that it <u>doesn't</u> work.

♥

I give up!

"*H*e's impossible! No matter how many times I try to tell him the same thing, he still does it his way. I give up!"

"I've tried over and over to please her. My reward is that she's angry at me all the time. I give up!"

You have to give these people credit – they're not easily discouraged. They try, fail, and try again. It's only after all reserves of energy and hope are exhausted that they finally throw in the towel.

I've read that a human being is one of the few creatures which will persist in a behavior that has demonstrated itself to be useless. When something has proven that it doesn't work, a person may keep trying it indefinitely. In an animal, the persistent failure of a behavior will effectively extinguish that behavior. (Like in those psychology experiments– if pushing the lever never gets the rat a food pellet, he stops pushing the lever and looks for something else to do to get food.)

Human beings are, in general, intellectually superior to animals. We can think about things in ways that animals cannot. This means that it's only in humans that a persistent belief that something should work can conquer experience that says that it doesn't work.

By the time you're part of an adult couple, you have accumulated a lot experience that teaches you how things work between people. This is one of those "relationship maps" I've described before. This sets up your expectations about how things should work. It's only natural to assume that what's worked before will work again. But not all maps can generalize – it may be appropriate in one situation or have been appropriate at one time and not be appropriate here or now. Once you have a map, it can be hard to think beyond its borders, to recognize that <u>should be</u> does not equal <u>is</u>. You have to be able to recognize the problem before you can reorganize your thinking to find a solution.

In the example above, Annie keeps telling Todd the same thing in the same way. It makes sense to her, so she figures it <u>should</u> make sense to him. In her interpretation of events, he's failing to respond appropriately to what <u>should</u> be the appropriate input. There's something wrong with him.

Todd has a clear sense of what <u>should</u> make Annie happy and he's doing it. In his interpretation of events, she's failing to respond appropriately to what <u>should</u> be the appropriate input. There's something wrong with her.

They both feel aggrieved because they have each been most persistent in applying what <u>should</u> be the appropriate input. Unfortunately, they've had difficulty reaching beyond their old maps. They're not remembering the basic navigation rule of relationship maps – "if it doesn't work, try something else." Even if you truly and absolutely believe that something <u>should</u> work, it's not very functional to persist when it clearly <u>isn't</u> working.

They both need to be appreciated by their partners for their committed persistence. They also need to be willing to open themselves up to new ways of operating, no matter how strongly they believe that what they were doing should have worked. It's simply not very helpful to label your partner defective and then give up.

For Annie, a new way of saying things to Todd might work. Perhaps she could use language that conveyed her internal experience in a way that carried no implications of accusation. That might help him to see past his own expectations of what she *should* be feeling.

As for Todd, his wish to take care of Annie is clear. An open-minded, nonjudgmental inquiry into her *actual* experience might produce the kind of information that he requires in order to create a response that will allow him to be more successful.

If these strategies don't succeed, there are others to try. When new behaviors prove successful, it's likely that they'll be repeated. It's necessary however to renew your commitment regularly to look beyond the old maps. It's important to see *what is* and to look for *what can be*. Maps can be used both to remind you about familiar territory and to help you maneuver through new territory. They're not meant to keep you stuck someplace ugly.

♥

There's ALWAYS a reason for behavior.

♥

There's always a reason

*L*et me tell you about my cat, Cletus. He is the most affection-ate cat I have ever met, in a long line of cats known. He obvi-ously loves me — he leaps up, even from a nap, at my presence. He reaches up to be held; and, when held, rubs against my face repeatedly. He purrs so loudly in my arms that I'm concerned about violating noise ordinances. He loves to be petted and scritched. The other day, when I was petting him in the conventional way, and he was purring in his normal effusive fashion, he suddenly, for no apparent reason, swiped out and clawed me. Boy, was I surprised (and bleeding)! I was hurt, physically and emotionally. And I was angry. "Stupid cat." Also, "Are you nuts?!"

It was only later that I discovered that he had been in a fight and that he had, among other wounds, a small but obviously ten-der wound on his back, hidden under a thick fur coat. Since I hadn't seen the wound, and of course he hadn't told me about it, I hadn't taken it into consideration in how I was petting him. I had, with no intention to do so, hurt him. He had retaliated. Since he is not otherwise apparently psychotic, I assume his intention was to stop me from repeating something hurtful. His intention, then, was not to hurt me but to keep me from hurting him.

Last week Lawrence came into my office complaining that Rilka, his wife, was, for no reason, mad at him and punishing him. I've worked with Rilka. She manifests no symptoms of insanity. And Lawrence would insist that she's not "crazy" in some clinical way, just that she lashes out at him for no reason.

So I told Lawrence, an animal lover, about my cat. When he was into the cat story, he spontaneously said, "You should have known that there was something going on for the cat — they don't suddenly hurt the people they love for no good reason. You should have looked for a sore spot right away. It's not like he can tell you where it hurts."

As I waited for the parallel between cats and people to settle into Lawrence's thinking, he started to frown.

"But people CAN tell you where it hurts," he said. So we talked about that.

It's certainly true that people have a facility with language that cats do not. But there can be lots of reasons why people can't or don't tell you where it hurts.

Rilka's sensitivity had its origins in the contemptuous and dismissive way that her grandmother had always addressed her while she was growing up. When Lawrence used a certain tone of voice with her, particularly if he was preoccupied with something else when he spoke to her, it was, for Rilka, a reliving of her dealings with her grandmother. Rilka, not being crazy, did not experience Lawrence as her grandmother. Grandmother had been dead for 5 years when Lawrence and Rilka had gotten married. It never occurred to her to discuss her history with her grandmother with her husband. She only knew that when he spoke to her "that way" she became instantly angry and defensive.

Lawrence had no such history with his parents or grandparents. He had no reason to suspect that such a wound existed in his wife. He'd never put together that his manner of speaking to her precipitated her angry outbursts. From his point of view, it was an unpredictable event, without rhyme or reason.

Together with Rilka, we talked in session about this series of events that was no longer camouflaged. Rilka was able now to discuss with Lawrence how *now-with-him* connected to *then-with-Grandmother*. With this new awareness of this sensitivity in place, Lawrence was able to look directly at his manner of speaking to Rilka. Although he was never able to understand why Rilka couldn't keep "now" and "then" separate in her reactions, he was no longer either unaware of the sensitivity or surprised at the reaction he got when he spoke to her in "that way". In fact, he was able for the most part to refrain from speaking to her in those ways that caused her pain. She was more secure in their interactions and grateful that he was willing and able to make the change for her. He was more successful as a husband and more comfortable now that he no longer had to fear unexpected and painful attacks.

They both now knew that there's ALWAYS a reason for behavior. When they came upon other such events between them, they knew to look for the sensitivities. The very act of posing the questions to each other represented a loving commitment to each other and to the relationship

♥

Maybe we all carry around a fear that
a partner could let us down.

♥

How could you even think that?!

*M*ariska picked up the ringing phone, and, after listening for a moment, said, "What are you talking about?" in a peevish tone. "I don't know anything about that; you'll have to speak to my husband," she said snappishly and put the receiver down with more than adequate force.

For the next hour, she stewed. The more she thought about it, the angrier she became. How could he have done something like that?! In the 17 years that they'd been married, they'd always made major decisions jointly. She had never just up and committed a sizeable chunk of money without even consulting Neil. And here he was apparently having made a decision to buy a new car, for heaven's sake, without even telling her! And that smug salesman! Obviously Neil had led him to believe that this was just fine and dandy with her. Or worse, had led him to believe that she was irrelevant! She was livid!

For the full hour until Neil got home, she cycled from hurt to insulted to enraged and around again. By the time Neil walked in the door, she'd gone past simmer to boil over. When he walked over to give her a "hello" kiss, she threw the message pad at him. It was too light to do any damage but it certainly surprised him.

"Mariska! What in the world has gotten into you?!"

She hissed at him, "It's from your dear friend, Whit. He says the car you wanted is ready whenever you are but that he has a few questions. Since I knew NOTHING about this, I couldn't help him out." She had her arms crossed over her chest and her jaw set so hard that it could have cracked walnuts.

Neil thought he should probably be defending himself, but he didn't have a clue about what the charges were. He did know however that he didn't like having things thrown at him.

"Mariska, unclench your jaw enough to tell me what you're angry about. And who in the world is 'Whit'?"

Mariska looked confused, but she wasn't ready to put down her arms, literally or figuratively. "Whit is the car salesman from whom you have apparently arranged to purchase your new car. A purchase that we have not agreed on, I would point out!"

"Whit must be that aggressive salesman that kept sidling up to me while I was walking around the lot on Saturday. Remember, when I took my car in to be serviced, you said I should look around because we'd need to replace my car sometime in the next few months. That little weasel must have gotten my name and number from the Service Department. What nerve!"

Mariska looked deflated. "You mean you didn't order a car without talking to me first?"

"Mariska, we've been married for 17 years. In all that time, have I ever done such a thing? Of course not. It really hurts to think that after all these years together you'd believe that I would do something like that." Neil walked out to the deck to get some fresh air.

After a few minutes, Mariska came out to the deck carrying two glasses of lemonade. She held one out as a peace offering.

"Neil, I should have known better. I'm sorry."

Neil took the lemonade but was still frowning. "I thought you knew me, really knew me. It's not just insulting, Mariska. It really hurts to feel that you may not know me after all this time together."

"Neil, I am so sorry to have hurt you. It was stupid of me to leap to a conclusion that flies in the face of everything I know about the man you are and the husband you've been. I think maybe we all carry around a fear that a partner could let us down. Look at Tom, who just found out that his wife's been having an affair for 2 years. And what about Lisa, who got served divorce papers out of the blue? But, I am sorry, Neil. You did nothing to deserve mistrust. Please forgive me."

Neil heard in Mariska's apology that she really did know him, even if she had lost sight of that for an hour or so. He could hear that she was sincere and that she had been scared, and his anger evaporated. He gave her a sideways smile and said, "So about that Porsche I've always wanted..."

Sometimes a minor event can touch us in some primal way that provokes a strong, even violent reaction. The reaction can be irrational, totally unpredicated on anything that has happened before. A partner can be left wounded and confused. The solution, as always, is communication. When partners bring feelings out into words and share them, the opportunity exists for any event to lead to greater understanding and greater closeness.

Before leaping to any conclusions, ask yourself if your history with your partner supports your fears. If the answer is "no", consider that running the fear and the questions past your partner, without accusation, creates an opportunity both to be reassured and to increase the level of understanding that exists between you and your partner. If you refrain from jumping to unwarranted conclusions, you also make a statement of faith in your partner. Such a statement is a powerful affirmation between people who care about each other.

♥

We all want to feel that what we do has an effect
on something or someone.

♥

Responding

*W*hen a toddler is hammering on a cobbler's bench, it isn't just about noise and percussion. Most fundamentally, it's about having a perceptible effect on something. He hammers the peg; it pushes out the other side. Something happens as a direct result of his action. In psychological terms, this is referred to as "efficacy". We all seek the experience of efficacy. We all want to feel and believe that what we do has an effect on something or someone. In a relationship, it becomes particularly compelling to feel that what we do or say has an effect on our partners. There is very little that is more disappointing than finding out that our words and actions are irrelevant to those people who mean the most to us.

Even if our partners have listened to us, even if they demonstrate that they understand us, it is nonetheless inadequate if that listening and understanding isn't followed by responding to us. We need to feel that having listened and understood, they want now to be responsive. Responsiveness, remember, doesn't require compliance or obedience. It requires that we observe that our partners have behaved, in word or deed, in some fashion that demonstrates that they have translated listening and understanding into action. We need to experience efficacy, to perceive that our actions have an effect on the people who are most important in our lives.

♥

Go into a relationship with the expectation that your partner is <u>not</u> going to change and the expectation that <u>you</u> are.

♥

Change

*T*here's an old joke – a woman marries a man hoping he'll change; a man marries a woman hoping she won't. The irony of course is that they're both wrong.

In a successful and healthy marriage, both people have to grow and become better people. But they don't become different people.

It's a bad plan to go into a marriage with the expectation that the behavior that you can't tolerate now is going to go away. It's an equally bad plan to go into marriage with the determination that you're not going to change "just" because your partner wants you to.

Go into a relationship with the expectation that your partner is <u>not</u> going to change and the expectation that <u>you</u> are. Be prepared to make compromises, to learn to do some things differently, to accept certain deviations from your customary ways of doing things.

Don't go any further into the relationship if what exists now in your prospective partner isn't good enough. Don't go any further into the relationship unless you're willing to evolve into a better person than you are now.

I remember a friend of mine telling me when she was pregnant with her first child that she was not going to let this baby change her lifestyle. She expected the baby to enhance her life but not change it. Hoo, boy! Many years and several children later, we do love to laugh at this story.

Marriage is a lot like this. We often enter marriage expecting it to enhance our lives but not to change us as people. It can't work both ways. It is possible to enter into a marriage and not change. But that marriage cannot be a strong and healthy marriage. Strong and healthy marriages endure because partners do change – from unencumbered individuals to partners. Partners by definition are encumbered by the needs of their partners and the needs of the relationship. You can refuse to be responsive to those needs; but the marriage will inevitably be weakened by that refusal.

Don't confuse your responsibility to grow and change with some privilege and magical capacity to change your partner. Your responsibility is to change yourself. Changing your partner is a delusion, and a frustrating one at that. You cannot change another person. The only person on this planet that you can change is yourself.

Enter a marriage affirming your partner for who he or she already is. Do not assume that what you want your partner to become is somehow implicit in his or her agreeing to marry you. He or she will not change.

Enter a marriage assuming that what you are now is only the beginning of what you will become. Enter it knowing that trying to meet your partner's needs is implicit in the agreement to marry. You will change.

Change – it's tricky business. It will surprise you when it does happen; it will surprise you when it doesn't.

♥

Women can teach men what kind of response they're looking
for
with a cue card.

♥

Cue cards

*O*ne of the real relationship challenges that exists for heterosexual couples is that women want to marry men but then expect men to converse like women. It's a communication conundrum. Heterosexual women are specifically looking to marry someone not-like them. Yet they often get very frustrated that their partners converse in ways that are not-like-them.

Men too get frustrated in this situation. They converse in the way that feels natural and familiar, the way that has been successful with other men. Then they find themselves failing in communication with their partners by behaving in this heretofore perfectly successful way. Another communication conundrum.

Men typically want to be successful in their communications with their partners. But they often have no idea how to get there from the familiar style that is not working for them in this context.

Enter the concept of "cue cards." The purpose of cue cards is to achieve success and happiness for both partners—happiness for women who are getting the kinds of conversational responses that they seek; success for men who are satisfying their partners' conversational needs.

Men often have no clue what kinds of responses their partners are looking for in a given conversation. What becomes clear very rapidly is that the kind of response that they might give other males in that context is thoroughly unsatisfactory to their female partners. It's unfair and unreasonable to get angry with men for giving male responses. On the other hand, for men to remain insistent that their usual way is the proper way when it's clearly an unsuccessful way is just silly and intransigent.

I'm suggesting that women, instead of getting disgusted, shift to an instructive posture. Teach men what kind of response you're looking for by using a cue card.

Men, instead of sticking to a losing strategy, be grateful for direction that points you to a successful strategy. See the cue card as your ticket to marital success.

Here's an example of how the cue cards can work to everyone's advantage—

Moira comes home from the meeting with her jaw clenched and a frantic gleam in her eye. Tom, astutely observing that she's looking very tense, asks, tentatively, if she'd like to talk about it.

Moira instantly launches into a litany of why committees are the devil's handiwork. Tom, wishing to be helpful, suggests that she quit the committee.

Instead of throwing up her hands in disgust and walking out on an unsatisfying exchange, Moira takes the opportunity to offer Tom a cue card. She tells him that what she's looking for here is sympathy not suggestions.

Tom, seizing on the cue card as his conversational salvation, immediately shifts to a sympathetic posture. After all, his only investment in this conversation is in being a good partner. Tom says, sympathetically, how frustrating it can be to be trapped in the slow and convoluted workings of a committee.

Moira, seeing Tom being so responsive to her stated need, is very touched by his commitment to her. She feels understood and supported; and she marvels at how intelligent and sensitive her husband is.

Tom feels unusually successful and revels in being appreciated.

The intention here has nothing to do with forcing an involuntary response from a partner, nor with faking a response. The critical principle is that both partners want to be successful and satisfied in this communication and relationship experience. The best way to get to that point is through respect.

Women need to respect that men arrive at the threshold of a relationship with a very different set of communication skills and experiences. Men are not always likely spontaneously to respond in the fashion desired by their women partners. This does not typically represent a failure of willingness but a deficit of understanding. Women can increase the likelihood that men respond in the desired way by teaching them, respectfully, what it is that they want to hear in a given circumstance. Offer cue cards.

Men need to receive, even seek, this instruction. This demonstrates a respect for their partners' needs. Ask for cue cards.

It's a conversational and relationship win-win.

♥

Responsiveness is taking understanding
and translating it into action.

♥

I can do that!

When you wanted to learn to ride a bike, you watched other kids doing it and thought how easy it looked. When you first got up on those 2 wheels, you wondered how others had ever mastered something so difficult. Then when you'd been riding for some time, you wondered how you'd ever found it so difficult. It seemed by then to come naturally. Well, is learning to ride a bike easy or hard? As with so many things, once you know what to do, doing it is relatively easy. But figuring out what to do can be hard.

When Sandy and Joyce started in marriage counseling, they were both pretty frustrated. Sandy considered Joyce impossible to please. No matter what he did, it was never good enough. Joyce was just as discouraged. Sandy seemed determined to make her angry and unwilling to work on their marriage. On their own they had found it impossible to figure out what to do. In fact, they didn't even recognize that the problem wasn't a failure of love or commitment but that neither one understood what the other needed and wanted.

In counseling they were helped to put into concrete terms what they needed from each other and from marriage. When Sandy heard from Joyce what she needed to feel loved and secure, he was suspicious – it seemed too easy.

For example, she needed to be kissed each morning when they parted to go to work. This gesture signified to her that he was promising to return. Since Sandy knew that he had every intention of returning each evening, he was puzzled as to why this was necessary or important to Joyce. In the therapy session, he was able to listen to Joyce explain how this gesture, or its absence, made her feel. He came to understand its importance to his wife, even though he frankly never could understand why. When asked if he could be responsive to his wife's need, even if he couldn't identify with the need, he said, "I can do that." But he said it with suspicion that something that he could do so easily could be so important.

Joyce never could imagine why Sandy didn't connect with this at an intuitive level. But she came to recognize that he really didn't. It wasn't stubbornness – he really didn't see it the same way that she did. She learned that just because something was obvious to her, that didn't mean that it was even a little bit obvious to Sandy. His "failure" to see things the way she did wasn't a reflection of a lack of caring. She had to give up her belief that there was only one obvious right way to see relationship issues. She started to take responsibility for teaching Sandy about her feelings instead of being angry that he didn't simply know how to meet her needs.

He actively invited this kind of communication with statements like, "I don't understand what this is about for you, but I would like to understand."

She shared with him without expecting him to understand automatically. She didn't treat his lack of understanding as a character flaw. Rather, she treated his inquiry as a statement of commitment to her, which was exactly what it was. She'd hang in there with him, looking for the right words to help him understand her experience.

Since what Joyce wanted and needed from him was not intuitive to Sandy, he had in the past frequently found himself trying to offer to her those things that made sense to him (but not to her). Since those gestures were not responsive to Joyce's actual needs, they of course failed to please her. In fact, they angered her because they were so far off the mark. When he tried harder, but with no input from her that he could make sense of, he only failed again.

He considered it part of his role and responsibility, as well as a source of pleasure, to make Joyce feel happy, loved, and secure. His persistent inability to succeed at this made him feel unappreciated, hopeless, and resentful. His anger at Joyce came, not from a failure of lovingness, but from an inability to succeed at something that was important to him because he did love her.

When he did understand her experience and her needs, he then demonstrated that he'd do his best to be responsive to her. He took his understanding and translated it into some kind of action. When he understood what to do, his success rate went up dramatically, of course.

The first step of the therapy was illuminating for them both their mutual commitments to each other. ("I want to do that.") The second was helping them to communicate— in terms that both could use productively— their feelings, needs, and wishes. ("This is what I need you to do.") The third was allowing them to demonstrate to each other, in more enlightened ways, those commitments. ("I can do that.")

Like riding a bike, when they found out what it took to succeed they could manage it. Just like riding a bike, as it became more practiced it felt more natural.

♥

A primitive need of the human spirit—
to feel attended to by another person.

♥

Attention!

A baby, being completely dependent and helpless, seeks at least one person who'll attend to its needs and wishes with absolute devotion. Although most, if not all, of the devotion received will be imperfect, it nonetheless will meet a most fundamental and primitive need of the human spirit – the need to feel attended to by another person.

We all, regardless of age, carry this need within us at all times. It is particularly activated by being in an emotionally intimate relationship with someone. Of all the wishes with which we arrive at a relationship, the most powerful may be the wish to feel that someone will offer us perfect devotion and attention.

A lucky baby looks into a parent's eyes and sees that parent looking attentively back. This is a response that carries a message: "I care, I'm here for you, I wish to do for you." No matter how mature you become, you never outgrow your need to receive that message from the emotionally important people in your life. A baby really is helpless and needs to have someone do just about everything. An adult is not helpless, but even when you <u>can</u> do most things for yourself, your emotional need to feel that someone <u>would</u> do things for you remains. You still want to receive that message of attentiveness.

A partner can send that message in many different ways. The most powerful is the simplest – eye contact. When you offer someone your undivided attention, that person feels once more that he or she is the center of the universe and is being attended to by someone devoted to his or her experience.

Beyond that, there are many different ways that people can feel attended to by the important people in their lives. One teenage girl

I know swears that the same food tastes better when her mom makes it for her than when she makes it for herself. It's not that she's trying to con her mom into waiting on her. The daughter's experience honestly is that the food tastes different. What she's responding to, in her brain rather than on her taste buds, is that when her mom cooks for her the meal feels like love, attention, and devotion.

Partners often experience similar events. The coffee that your partner brings you in the morning may be objectively no different from the cup that you'd make yourself. It may taste better because it carries a message of attentiveness along with its caffeine.

Having your partner take over, even temporarily, a task that you find unpleasant – driving your mom to the podiatrist, making cookies for the fund-raiser – feels much bigger than just getting out of the actual task. It feels like that attentiveness that we're all seeking. It says that someone paid enough attention to your wishes and needs to know that this would be a welcome gift. Then that person cared enough to give the gift. Even if you were perfectly capable (if unenthusiastic) about the task, it feels like you're being attended to when your partner does it for you. The gift then carries this extra value of meeting a primitive need that we all carry within us.

An important key to making this attentiveness work successfully in a relationship is finding out what counts as "good" attention to your partner. For example, for one person, being checked on regularly when he's sick feels good and attentive. For his wife, being checked on regularly when she's sick feels suffocating and irritating. *A proper gift is that which pleases the recipient.* We chuckle when Dennis the Menace gives his mom a football for her birthday because that's what <u>he</u> wants. It's not so amusing when your partner gives you what he or she would like to receive instead of what it is that <u>you</u> want. The husband who likes to be fussed over when he's sick may have the very loving impulse to fuss over his wife when she's sick. The truly loving and attentive act, however, is to do for her what <u>she'd</u> appreciate, which in this case is the opposite of his impulse.

Attention is such a basic need of people, and the need is triggered so powerfully in intimate relationships, that it holds tremendous power to define a relationship as either successful or unsuccessful. The energy that you put into making your partner feel attended to will be repaid many times over. Similarly, any stinginess in the attention that you pay to your partner will cost you dearly in your partner's sense of how well this relationship is working.

♥

If you experience your partner as attending to
<u>your</u> emotional needs, then it becomes possible
for you to attend to your partner's needs.

♥

Self vs. other

*J*ack and Maureen had been married less than a year. They were in their late 30s and partnership was new to both of them. They'd fallen deeply in love with each other and the decision to marry had been a no-brainer. But as they bumped into the daily little potholes of two people sharing intimate space, they were each starting to wonder about priorities. How did you balance taking care of yourself against taking care of your partner?

One of the engaging questions in psychology is that of self-interest vs. altruism. Which is the prime directive for people – doing for self or doing for others? Taking care of your own needs or taking care of another person's needs?

Many years ago a psychologist named Abraham Maslow described a hierarchy of needs. Needs ranged from the most primitive need (physical survival) to the most complex (self-actualization). A very important concept was that of hierarchy: that things are arranged in a specific order, with some higher than others. Only after the most basic needs were addressed was a person able to move on to attempt to meet higher level needs. For example, it was only after a caveman had fed himself that he might indulge his creative impulses in cave art.

I propose that, within relationships, a similar hierarchy exists. Just as within Maslow's hierarchy, individual survival must first be assured. Only when there is a secure sense of individual safety can a partner move beyond this basic need to attend to other higher level needs, like nurturing a partner or a relationship.

Whereas Maslow was talking about physical survival, I'm talking about emotional survival. Human beings require certain things within relationships in order to feel that their emotional survival is assured. This includes respect, affection, commitment, trust, and a feeling that you're a priority for your partner. These may not be all that is necessary between any particular two people, but they're likely to be a minimum for a successful relationship.

When someone feels that one or more critical ingredients are missing in a relationship, then all energy will be diverted to emotional survival. When someone feels that the fundamentals are taken care of, then psychic energy can be redirected to nurturing a partner.

For example, Maureen wasn't confident that her new husband, Jack, would behave in a loving way towards her 10 year old poodle. Whenever Jack and the poodle were in the same room, Maureen tended to sit between them with her arm around the dog. Maureen was taking care of the dog, of course. But she was also taking care of her own emotional safety.

She'd loved and been committed to the dog long before she met Jack, so anything that hurt the dog, hurt her. Jack, recognizing that the dog was a basic issue for Maureen, committed himself to becoming friends with the poodle. He consistently treated the dog with respect and affection, even bringing home little doggie treats. When Maureen saw Jack's caring behavior towards the dog, she could relax her protective posture (emotionally as well as physically). She understood at some level that he was making a powerful statement about being sensitive to her and those things important to her. When she saw that <u>he</u>'d take care of the dog, then <u>she</u> could divert her energy to the next higher need – Jack.

When Jack took care of Maureen's need, Maureen was freed to take care of Jack. She responded to Jack's behavior by being loving and sensitive to Jack's needs. In particular, she was very solicitous of his needs and feelings whenever he came home from a visit to his elderly parents. The visits always upset him, and he was particularly grateful that at those times Maureen made herself available with hugs and a sympathetic ear to hear his anxieties and sadness.

By attending to Maureen's emotional needs, Jack freed Maureen to direct her energy away from self-protection and toward his needs.

Some generally applicable rules of relationships, then, are these:

Once your own emotional safety is taken care of, your energy is available to be directed to your partner's needs.

If you experience your partner as attending to your emotional needs, then it becomes possible for you to attend to your partner's needs.

To the degree that you feel that your partner actively <u>wishes</u> to attend to your needs, you'll feel that attending to your partner's needs is a pleasure rather than a burden.

The answer to the question then of whether people are basically selfish or altruistic depends on the circumstances. In physical terms, living organisms will generally attempt to ensure their own survival. Once that's accomplished, then higher level goals can be addressed (like worrying about creative expression).

In relationship terms, if the selfish goal of emotional safety has been met, then the altruistic goal of tending to a partner's needs can be addressed. The two aren't necessarily contradictory. In fact, once the mechanisms are understood, the hierarchy acts like a road map to help shed light on complex relationship terrain.

♥

<u>How</u> two people come to a decision will
determine if the outcome "works".

♥

Agreeing to disagree isn't always good enough

*M*arvin says, "I've been thinking about Italian all day; I can already taste those meatballs."

Cynthia says, "Wait a minute. I've had my heart set on Chinese; I've been waiting all day for my egg roll."

What they end up eating is "outcome". How they get to the decision is "process". So, which is more important? Is it the final answer that matters or is it how you get there? In relationships, this is a trick question.

As is obvious, couples will not always agree on everything. The divergences can happen on anything from the least important (like where to have dinner) to the most important (like whether to have children). What becomes clear in working with couples is that even the least important issue can become hugely troublesome in a relationship if you feel that you're not getting the kind of response that you need from your partner.

Let's take something that most people would probably agree is a relatively small question, like whether dinner tonight will be at the usual Italian or the usual Chinese restaurant.

What about Marvin and Cynthia? We have clearly competing directions here. What would constitute the "best" resolution? Lots of outcomes are possible, but they all accomplish different things.

Marvin and Cynthia could go their separate ways for dinner and each get what they want to eat. That accomplishes menu but does nothing for togetherness.

They could eat at a food court, which would allow them to be together and each get the menu item they crave (but in a mediocre environment, and not really the restaurant they each want).

Either could "give in" to the other, accomplishing togetherness, with one of them getting exactly the food he or she wants and the other not at all.

So, which is the right way to do it? Yes, another trick question. We can't know yet which is the "right" outcome. The process comes first. How two people come to a decision will determine if the outcome "works". *Almost any outcome can be acceptable if both people believe that their feelings were considered by a partner to whom those feelings were important.*

One way to do it horribly wrong is to try to persuade your partner that s/he doesn't really want what s/he thinks s/he wants. Cynthia might try to persuade Marvin that he doesn't really want Italian with meatballs, maybe because he's watching his red meat intake. She may well succeed in getting him to give up on the Italian restaurant for tonight. He may even go along with Chinese ("Sure, fine, whatever."), but the process was lousy. She got the outcome she wanted by making Marvin feel bad. They may eat together, but they'll be farther apart.

On the other hand, Cynthia could tell Marvin how much she's craving that eggroll. She could promise that if he goes along with Chinese for tonight, she'll enthusiastically support Italian whenever he next wants it. She could ask for his generosity on this, as opposed to presenting it as something he *should* or *must* do. All of these things communicate to Marvin that his feelings are important to her, even as she asks that he accommodate to her wishes. If he does agree to Chinese, her sincere "thank you" also lets him feel that his gesture is appreciated.

Marvin may end the evening a little disappointed that he didn't get those meatballs, but he won't be angry or hurt or resentful. He'll feel respected and considered even though he didn't get the meal that he'd hoped. The process will feel good even if the outcome wasn't his first choice. And when Cynthia makes a point of suggesting Italian the next time eating out comes up, Marvin will feel affirmed in believing that his wishes matter to his partner.

Feeling considered and cared about is much more important than menu, or most of the other gazillion things about which partners may disagree.

♥

By acting with good grace, he has
demonstrated responsiveness and affirmed
his commitment to this relationship.

♥

Go along graciously

*F*red is getting his briefcase ready for the next morning. He's thinking through the day ahead, imagining which files he'll need, checking through his list of appointments and meetings. He's acutely aware that the evening is slipping away from him and he still has a lot to do for the big meeting in the morning.

Kelly calls downstairs, "Honey, would you mind helping Nicky with his spelling words before he goes to bed?"

What we have here is a challenge and an opportunity. Fred is surely being challenged – he wants and needs to continue working on <u>his</u> stuff. He's feeling the time crunch, knowing he has to have everything organized before he leaves the house at the crack of dawn to make that breakfast meeting. And he's right in the middle of thinking through all the details. He doesn't want to shift mental gears to work on 3rd grade spelling. As an individual, he rebels at the idea of stopping what's he doing in order to accede to someone else's wishes. After all, his individual needs are legitimate too.

As a partner in a successful relationship, he understands that his needs, legitimate or not, have to be balanced against another person's needs. He's sure that Kelly knows that he has a lot to do to prepare for tomorrow. He knows that she isn't quick to pawn off work on others. But he doesn't really know why this is being put on his plate. He could refuse. He could ask, "Do I have to?" He could just say, "Yes." He wrestles with himself as he confronts the challenge that asks who'll be victorious – Fred, the individual, or Fred, the partner?

As he thinks about it, he quickly realizes that Fred, the partner, is going to call the shots on this one. He's going to do what Kelly has asked of him. But he's not thrilled about it and wants her to know that. His impulse is to say, "Yes," but in a grumpy way that communicates his displeasure at being interrupted.

He gives it further thought. If he says a grumpy yes, he'll make his displeasure clear, but he'll probably look selfish and he's likely to make Kelly angry with him for being so uncooperative. So, he'll end up interrupted, doing what she asked instead of what he wants, and in the doghouse anyway. Stupid plan.

He reconsiders. There's an opportunity here as well. If he's going to do it anyway, why not get credit for being a good team player? If he's going to do it, he's going to do it with good grace. That way he'll earn good partner points by putting aside his needs to help Nicky AND he'll get to keep all the points that he earns. He's thought through this conflict before and come to think of this way of resolving it as "doing it with style."

He calls up to Kelly, "Sure, Hon; I'll be right there."

Fred has converted this challenge into the opportunity to be a responsive partner. By acting with good grace, he has demonstrated responsiveness and thereby affirmed his commitment to this relationship. (You may recognize that Fred has made a significant deposit into the emotional bank account of this relationship. This will turn out to be very useful when he calls home the next day to say that he has to work late and won't be home for his turn to make dinner.)

As they settle down into bed that night, Kelly kisses him and thanks him for taking care of Nicky's spelling so graciously. Fred just smiles and says, "No problem." He's no dummy. He knows that this is not the moment to discuss whether he should have been asked to help with this tonight. There will be other times to talk about how pressured he feels before these breakfast meetings.

At the moment, he's just going to drift off to sleep basking in the glow of being appreciated.

♥

The hurt and the rage are as big as the emotional investment.

♥

"Givers of pain and delight"

"**N**obody can make me as happy as he can. And no one can make me as furious either!"

"How can she make me want to protect her from the world one minute and want to strangle her the next?"

One of the indications of a powerful bond between people is this experience of moving from one emotional extreme to the other. When someone has the ability to make you deliriously happy, it seems downright vicious when they instead make you miserable. Sometimes it can feel like your partner is willfully withholding something that's important to you.

Except for rare circumstances, people <u>want</u> their partners to have what they want and need. It's particularly gratifying to be the one to provide those things. But sometimes people become so lost in trying to protect their own interests that they lose sight of how and why to take care of their partner's.

How does this happen? Generally, the more you feel that your own interests are not being taken care of by someone else, the more you feel that you must make it your priority to take care of them yourself. On the other hand, as we discussed earlier, the more you feel that your partner considers your interests a priority, the more able you are to shift your focus to their needs and wishes.

This presents a paradox – your partner is more likely to meet *your* needs to the degree that your partner believes that you're committed to meeting *his or her* needs.

When your partner believes that you could meet his or her needs but you're choosing not to, the response is hurt and rage.

Your partner's thinking, "Here you have the power to give delight, and you choose instead to give pain." When this happens between people with a powerful bond, the result is also powerful – the hurt and the rage are as big as the emotional investment. The more you're able to bring delight to your partner, the more painfully it registers if you "fail" to do so.

As with any wounded creature, the response to pain will be self-protection. If you're busy defending yourself and protecting your own interests, then you're unlikely to have energy or interest left over for attending to anyone else's needs.

Imagine if you could interrupt this sequence early. Imagine if at the very beginning you could say, "Hold on here. If I have the power to make you happy by providing something you want and need, I'd like to be able to do that. Here's what *I* need to be able to give you what *you* need."

Henry's scared because his company is downsizing. Each evening, instead of walking with Suzanne, as usual, he's been coming home and brooding over a few beers. Suzanne misses him severely. Their walks had been a prime source for her of connection time with Henry and of time to process verbally her own day. Each evening that he opts out of their walk makes her feel more abandoned and more angry. When Henry is ready one evening about two weeks later to share his fears with Suzanne, she tells him that she's unavailable. She's made plans with a friend to walk that evening. Henry's crushed that she'd desert him when he needs her. He calls a buddy and announces to Suzanne that he's planned an evening of beer and poker.

Suzanne's hurt and anger about Henry's withdrawal was as big as her emotional connection to him. She depended on those walks and when he took them away from her, she felt that he was being willfully unkind and insensitive. If he wasn't going to take care of her needs, she'd just have to do it for herself. If she was doing that, she couldn't simultaneously be available to him for his needs.

Henry too depended on their walks. It had taken him two weeks to get his feelings in sufficient order to be able to bring them to Suzanne. When he was ready, it felt to him like she'd abandoned him. Needing to do something with those feelings and finding Suzanne unavailable, he took his hurt and anger and looked for an alternative way to take care of himself.

Feeling that a partner was willfully unavailable to them, each of them was hurt and angry. When it appeared that each of them would have to meet their own needs independently, they took the energy that would have been available to the partner and applied it to their own needs. Instead of taking care of each other, now they were taking care of themselves.

The dimension of their hurt and anger was an index of the dimension of their emotional bond. If they could find their way back to it, that same emotional bond could be called on to find a more satisfactory solution to their impasse, By reconnecting with that bond, they could find the will to look for solutions within the marriage.

As they started, tentatively, to talk about what they were feeling and how much they each missed their walks, they reconnected with their mutual wish for closeness and connection. They discovered that they both actually wanted to be able to be there for each other. Each of them had to be convinced of their partner's desire for this though. Once each of them felt their partner's commitment, each of them could leave their own needs in their partner's care and turn their attention to taking care of their partner.

They found in their bond the ability to discuss what they each needed to have in order to be able to give of themselves generously. This allowed them to negotiate a win-win solution to their respective needs and fears. Both got to be givers of delight. No one had to get pain.

♥

I really loved the person that I married...
I miss that person so badly.

♥

I hate you because I love you

*S*he rounded on him with a red-hot fury that simply blazed from her eyes. She spat out the words as they fought; and every accusation she made seemed only to feed her rage. Her fury finally spent, she clenched her jaw and went up to bed without a backward glance, slamming and locking the bedroom door behind her.

He felt like he'd been mauled. The hate in her tone just blew him away. How could anyone be that angry with her husband, the father of her children? As he reeled, he found himself unaccountably thinking back to their wedding day. Wow. It seemed like another reality. He could recall that time without difficulty. He could see her face as he lifted her veil, the radiance of her smile as she looked into his eyes. They'd been absolutely sure about how much they loved each other, about wanting to be together forever. How does anyone get from that to this?

The next few days were spent in chilly coexistence. By the weekend, he detected a slight thaw after they'd spent the day together as a family. No matter what was going on between them as a couple, they were always able to come together as parents and enjoy their kids. He knew she thought he was a great dad and he thought she was a wonderful mom.

After the kids were in bed, he brought her a cup of tea and a single red rose that he'd bought that afternoon and hidden in anticipation of this moment. It was something he used to do all the time. To his surprise, she burst into tears. He stammered out an apology for making her cry (though he had no idea why she was crying), and she just waved it away. Though confused, he had the sense to remain quiet while she cried.

When her tears were finished, she tried to explain them.

"I really loved the man that I married, the man who used to bring me roses at the drop of a hat. He was my best friend as well as my lover. When we got married, I was looking forward to at least fifty years with that man."

"So how could you tell me, scream at me, the other night that you hate me?"

"Because you've stolen that man away from me and I hate you for that."

His brow furrowed and he tried desperately to make sense of what she had said, but the best response he could manage was, "Huh?"

"That man was sensitive and kind. He always asked about my day and my feelings, my thoughts and my dreams. He listened to me as if I were the only person on the planet and the only thing that he cared about. He made me feel like a queen. He was never too tired to make love or too distracted to make conversation. He was fun and funny. He made me feel like the center of his universe. I loved that; I loved him; and I miss those things so badly." She started to cry again, but caught her breath enough to whisper that he'd stolen that man and she wanted him back.

He was struggling with these images. He started to defend himself, explaining that he was working so hard to make the kind of life that he wanted for them, that he was dancing as fast as he could, that it was all for them.

"Don't you understand? It's all for you and the kids. I admit that sometimes I'm a little distracted, and maybe I get grumpy. But it'll all pay off in the end; you'll see."

She looked defeated and sad when she said, "See? That's the man I hate. He steals away my husband and replaces him with this guy who thinks that being truly together can wait while he does other things. You're stealing my husband and using him up and all you leave for me is an empty, exhausted shell that looks like my husband but whose mind is elsewhere. Well, no thanks. It's worse than not having him at all."

As she stood up wearily to go upstairs alone, he stopped her. He reached out and took her hand, cupped her chin in his hand and looked straight into her eyes. It was more intimate than they'd been in ages.

"I'd like to try again. I want my option on those fifty years. Will you give me another chance?"

She wasn't confident that he could do it, but she knew how much she wanted it, so she nodded, "yes".

It takes a lot of communication to get from this point of agreement all the way to mutual understanding, and then from there to responsive behavior change. They're going to have to listen to each other, work hard at understanding experiences that are alien to their world views, and then engage in modifying their own behaviors while being patient with their partners' attempts to do the same. The whole operation will be made possible, although not necessarily easy, by their repeated reaffirmations of love and caring. When they reconnect with why they got married in the first place, their courage and stamina in the face of difficult work will be renewed.

♥

Complaining well can be constructive
and actually make a relationship better.

♥

Silence is golden ... NOT!

*T*he tale is as classic and familiar as *Cinderella*, but without the happy ending. Mick and Melinda had been married for 15 years. The marriage had started out well, loving and romantic. They'd loved so much about each other. Melinda had adored Mick from the moment they'd had their first date. She had been thrilled to be married to him. It had been easy to stay silent in those moments in which he disappointed or offended her, hurt her feelings, or said something worrisome. She had just let it pass, without comment. She'd figured it was silly to fuss about the small stuff; better to save your energy, and the relationship's, for the really big issues.

It's a common belief; and it's wrong. Evidence gathered by psychologist John Gottman and his "Marriage Clinic", for example, is quite clear – it's critical to the ultimate success (and survival) of a marriage for the partners to share their negative experiences of the relationship. And they must do so early, when the issues are small and current. The impulse to squelch the small complaints in the interest of long term congeniality is misguided. And the results are predictably bad.

When Melinda had stifled her feelings, she had become increasingly resentful of Mick. There were recurrent offenses, all without redress. After all, since he'd not heard from her what the offense was, he'd had no timely opportunity to make a repair. When they'd fought, accumulated offenses would come boiling out of Melinda, aimed squarely at Mick's head, and heart. Without timely input from Melinda, Mick was clueless about what she was feeling or what he'd needed to do differently to make her feel good about the relationship. Feeling attacked and a failure, Mick was constantly on the defensive. It was as if he'd walked into the middle of a fight, with no warning that Melinda was so angry or why. The recurrence of these outbursts was demoralizing and he too had become resentful.

Melinda and Mick had slowly drifted apart. Since Melinda was working from a rule that directed her not to address the problems unless they were immediately catastrophic, she'd kept getting quieter and quieter in the relationship, increasingly hopeless, withdrawing further and further from Mick. Mick, feeling cut off from her feelings and a persistent failure in his marriage, had felt frustrated and helpless to change what he didn't understand, and had withdrawn further and further from Melinda. Slowly, their affection for one another was defeated by their disconnection. They were too far apart to see the possibility to reach out to each other; and they no longer remembered why to bother. They eventually parted without rage, with disinterest, and with no remnant of the original affection or passion. Unlike Cinderella and her Prince Charming, this romance ended up a grim fairy tale —death by silence.

The principle of ignoring minor problems even shows up in book titles – like, "Don't sweat the small stuff". For purposes of dealing with <u>yourself</u>, this recommendation may have merit. For dealing with your partner, it's a killer. It generally, however, comes from good intentions. No one wants to be, or to be thought of as, a nag, a whiner, or a constant critic.

So, how do you manage to address things in a timely way and yet not be a pain in the butt? *How* you present your complaint, feeling, or issue goes a long way to determining how your partner responds to it.

By following these guidelines, the dangers of disconnection are avoided without introducing the dangers inherent in criticism or attack. Connection, while sometimes heated and complicated, creates the potential for growth together. Silence, while simple and seemingly harmless, gradually smothers the strong feelings that partners need in order to persist in creating successful bonding. It can feel very risky to bring up "the bad stuff". It turns out that the greater risk is in not bringing it up. But it's also possible to bring it up in ways that contribute to the health and warmth of a relationship rather than doing damage to the connection that already exists.

Here are some basic rules –

♥Avoid words like "always" or "never". They carry a message of criticism of your partner's overall functioning as a partner.

♥Stick to a discussion of today's events only (a rule made easier to follow if you haven't been storing up complaints like a squirrel stores nuts).

♥Start off the discussion with something positive, a comment about something your partner's been doing right (or at least more right than before, or with perceptible effort to be more right than before).

♥Be as concrete as possible in describing what it is that you want to be different and how you need it to be.

♥Say it once, clearly, and let it be; don't go on and on in an effort to make your point.

♥Give your partner a chance to ask questions.

♥Answer those questions with trust that your partner really wants to understand what it is that you want and need.

♥When your partner demonstrates effort to be responsive to your feelings, demonstrate appreciation. "Thank you" goes a long way toward making your partner feel successful.

Complaining well can be constructive and actually make a relationship better. A slow death from the asphyxiation of silence is a painful and horribly disappointing way to go.

♥

When your mom told you that "please" and "thank you" are
magic words,
she was right.

♥

Love is . . . saying, "Thank you"

*B*ill says, "I always hear about what I did wrong. I never hear about what I did right. What's the point of even trying?" Naturally, Bill then proceeds to invest less energy in trying to please his wife and looks for someplace else to achieve more likely success.

Lorraine says, "He doesn't appreciate anything I do. Does he think that the laundry fairy puts clean socks in his drawer?" Naturally, Lorraine then thinks it's not worth her effort to deliver clean laundry and proceeds to put that energy into something more rewarding for herself.

What went wrong here? Both these people had some level of investment in pleasing their partners, yet both have been frustrated in their hopes of getting something positive back for their efforts.

> *Among the most basic laws of behavior are these:*
>
> ♥   Behavior which is reinforced is likely to be repeated.
>
> Θ Behavior which isn't reinforced is less likely to be repeated.
>
> Ø Behavior which is punished is less likely to be repeated.

Reinforcement can take many forms. The key is that it's something that the person experiences as positive. It can be something pleasurable (a kiss), something valuable (a gift), etc. It can even be making something unpleasant stop (when he smokes less, her complaining stops). Anything that the person experiences as positive can serve as reinforcement. When any form of reinforcement follows a behavior, it will make that behavior more likely to be repeated. (That's why the teacher gave your child a gold star when she handed in her homework.)

But the other part is that if a behavior is followed by no reinforcement, it's less likely to repeat. (That's why you ignored your son instead of giving in when he whined for more TV.) If a behavior is followed by an unpleasant experience, it's also less likely to be repeated. (That's why you took away her video games when your daughter sneaked cookies before dinner.)

For example, Bill remembers that his wife likes the kitchen trash taken out immediately after dinner. Without waiting to be asked, he takes the trash out. If his wife fails to comment on this, then there's been no reinforcement of this desirable behavior. If in fact she makes a negative comment (like, "It's about time!"), then this desirable behavior has been followed by a punishing experience. As the laws of behavior state, this desirable behavior is now less likely to be repeated. Bill's wife has blown a chance to get something that she wants done in the future (the trash taken out after dinner).

If, on the other hand, Bill's trash removal is followed promptly by a pleasant "thank you", then Bill's action has been followed by a pleasing and reinforcing consequence. He feels that his efforts were both noticed and appreciated. These things make him feel worthwhile and valuable. This affirmation of his value is very positive and is therefore reinforcing. His reinforced behavior will be more likely to be repeated in the future.

People are sometimes amazed and incredulous that the simple act of thanking someone can be so powerful. Why is it so reinforcing? First, a thank you demonstrates that someone has noticed your action. This implies that your behavior was worthy of notice. It recognizes that, at least at that moment, you have some degree of importance to someone. As human beings, our self-esteem is strengthened by having an effect on someone. A thank you says explicitly that your action was valued by someone. Being noticed AND being valued is a very affirming experience.

Being noticed and appreciated are very positive and therefore very reinforcing. As the laws of behavior state, any action which is followed by reinforcement is likely to be repeated. This particular form of reinforcement is so personally affirming that it's especially potent. When such an experience is shared between people who have an investment in each other, it has a powerful bonding effect.

When you were growing up and your mom told you that "please" and "thank you" were magic words, she was right. Saying a sincere "Thank you" now has a magical influence on your partner's future behavior.

♥

You're sorry that the other person is unhappy
or that an unfortunate event has occurred.

♥

I'm sorry

When somebody dies, we often offer condolences by saying, "I'm so sorry for your loss." What exactly do we mean by this statement? We are not apologizing for causing the deceased's death. We pretty much never believe that we are responsible for his or her death. So, what are we sorry for? We're sorry that this person to whom we're offering condolences is feeling bad, sad, and bereaved. We're acknowledging that there are unhappy feelings and that we wish that the recipient of our wishes wasn't unhappy. In fact, even if we're just as happy that the old so-and-so is gone, we're still saying that we're sorry that the survivor is experiencing unhappiness.

When you're strolling down the street or through the mall and you bump into somebody going the other way, you probably reflexively respond with, "I'm sorry," or perhaps, "Excuse me." Did you stop to reflect first on whether you were responsible for the collision? Probably not. On the possibility that you in some way contributed to it, even if unintentionally, you simply offered the most basic apology. In all likelihood, you in no way felt diminished by the apology. It was the most fundamental courtesy to accept that you might have been party to the event even without recognizing how.

Let's see how this might play out in a relationship–

As Cathy walked into the house carrying an armful of books from the car, Jacob looked up from the table where he was paying bills and asked if he could help her. She smiled, said a heartfelt, "Thanks; there's more in the car," and went to put her stack of books away. Half an hour later, she walked into the living room and found him back at the bills, with all of the rest of the books neatly piled on the table.

"Where are the groceries?" she asked.

He frowned, puzzled, and said, "What groceries?"

She grimaced and said, "The ones from the car, of course. Don't tell me that they're still in there busily thawing. I thought you said that you'd bring them in." Her tone made it clear that she felt that he'd been remiss.

Jacob's first instinct was to defend himself from what felt like an attack. It was a particularly unexpected attack, too, since he had been anticipating a warm smile of appreciation when Cathy saw how he'd brought in all the books and made nice, neat piles for her.

He could have pointed out the piles. He could have pointed out that she'd never told him about any groceries. He would have been happy to bring in the groceries if he'd known they were there.

Instead, he said, "I'm sorry, honey. I didn't realize that there was anything else in the car besides books. Would you like me to get them now?"

Was Jacob saying that it was his fault that the groceries thawed? No. Truthfully, he didn't believe that it was his fault. He was perfectly confident that his intention had been to help in whatever way Cathy needed his help. On the other hand, he was aware that somehow there had been a communication breakdown. He wasn't sure if or how he had contributed to it, but he nonetheless regretted the outcome. He was, in fact, sorry that it hadn't worked out that he was as helpful as he had intended.

He was also sorry for Cathy's frustration as she saw that her efforts were now wasted because of the oversight. She'd worked so hard and now the ruined groceries would have to be shopped for all over again.

He wasn't claiming fault; he was expressing that he was sorry that an unfortunate event had occurred. He was also accepting that he might have in some unintended way contributed to this unfortunate result.

His "I'm sorry", however simple, was a pretty potent and positive response. Instead of explaining to him how it was all his fault,

Cathy now thanked him for his offer to retrieve the groceries. She felt supported and cared about. His easy apology left her feeling that he was her ally. The groceries were no less ruined, but the relationship was strengthened, all because Jacob gave her no less than the same courtesy that he would have given a stranger he bumped into on the street.

We so often get stingy with "I'm sorry" when it's with someone with whom we are emotionally intimate. Because of our emotional vulnerability in a relationship, instead of the impulse to offer the courtesy of those two simple words we often experience instead the impulse of self-defense. Instead of buying us more safety, though, it actually provokes a downward spiral of recrimination and more defense. Paradoxically, the attempt to avoid blame elicits that very blame from your partner. Conversely, the simple expression of "I'm sorry" strengthens the alliance and actually deflects any attempt to assign blame.

Whether with a stranger or an intimate, "I'm sorry" is generally the best way to respond to a perceived offense. The details can be worked out later as necessary.

♥

If you're not willing to be equally responsible for thinking, remembering, and planning, then you're not an equal partner.

♥

Equal partners

*I*t's not about who does which household tasks. It's not about earning equal money toward the household accounts. It's not about which weighs more in the labor equation, for example, mowing or ironing. It's not about whose body is doing more/better/easier work.

It's about thinking and feeling.

Who thinks about what has to be done? Who feels responsible for making sure things that need to be done get done?

Partners who say, "Just tell me what to do," are missing the point of being an equal partner. They may be legend in song and story for how hard they work and how they never flinch from the unpleasant tasks. But the respect that comes from being "equal" rests on the partner being perceived as feeling just as <u>responsible</u> for thinking ahead to what has to be done.

No matter how hard you're willing to work, if you're not willing to be responsible for thinking, remembering, and planning, then you're not equal. Your partner is carrying you.

A division of labor, including who's responsible for what, can be perfectly legitimate in a relationship. The key is that it has to be mutually agreed upon, fair and acceptable to both partners. For example, a planned, discussed outcome like this – "I'll worry about meals if you worry about the cleaning"; or "I'll do investments if you do savings," can work well.

A de facto division that evolves out of one party assuming the responsibility because the other partner doesn't is NOT a just division. "I'll stay on top of paying our bills or they won't get paid," or "I'll monitor how the kids do in school, because you just don't notice," is not okay – it grows out of the desperate need for <u>somebody</u> to take charge of a critical operation.

Consider your situation. If you cannot honestly say that there is a well-examined, mutually acceptable division of labor that exists in your household, take the opportunity NOW to have the necessary conversations with your partner. If you're the one who's been skating the responsibilities, admit your error and commit yourself to a fair and equitable, mutually respectful negotiation. If you feel that you've been carrying more than your fair share, talk to your partner about how you'd like it to be instead. Sometimes each partner may feel that he or she is already carrying too much of the burden.

The details of the outcome of a negotiation are generally less important than the fact that the negotiation takes place and is well resolved. "Well resolved" means that both parties feel well listened to and respected. It may be that a different division of labor is needed, or that an honest sharing of feelings about responsibilities is due. "Equal partners" does not mean that each person gets the same number of household jobs. It does mean that thinking about household tasks and feeling responsible for their accomplishment is fairly shared.

♥

"Just tell me what to do" is not adequate
partner participation.

♥

Just tell me what to do

Sometimes we mistakenly believe that a willingness to comply is adequate participation. If you're waiting for instruction, does that mean that your partner is the one in charge? It's lonely at the top, and sometimes a little scary to be all alone up there. Mostly, people want their partners to be "equal", meaning that you are able to rest assured that your partner is exercising as much initiative as you are to meet the demands and challenges of the situation. It means that you can rely on your partner to feel just as responsible for problem-solving as you are.

It was a rough morning in the Porfoy household. The five year old was missing a shoe and the two year old wouldn't leave for pre-school without her granola bar and juice box. Vic had gotten himself ready for work and come downstairs to find both kids in tears and Doris running around the house while yelling to the kids to stop crying and stay at the front door.

Vic put down his briefcase and tracked down Doris.

"Hi, Honey. Things seem crazy down here. Just tell me what to do to help you." He was trying to put on his most calming and loving voice and most cooperative attitude. Imagine his surprise when Doris, instead of looking deeply grateful for his help, turned her head and snapped, "Well, as soon as I have a moment I'll write you a list!" She went back to searching and yelling and ignored him completely.

Vic was confused. He picked up his briefcase and went to work, knowing that he'd messed up the morning but puzzled about how a sincere offer to help could have been offensive.

When Vic got home, he found a snarling wife. Summoning his courage, he asked straight out what he'd done wrong that morning.

"That's the point, Vic, isn't it? You're waiting for me to explain it to you."

"Doris, help me out here. I really don't know and I really want to know. I just wanted to help you out this morning and you bit my head off."

Doris, seeing that he was willing to pursue this even in the face of her anger, decided that his intentions were honorable. She took a slow, deep breath and calmed herself down enough to explain.

"Vic, Mary couldn't find her shoe and Patty wanted her snack stuff. There was nothing mysterious about what needed to be done. Why in the world did you need my instructions for how to be helpful? You're a grown-up. You know perfectly well what has to be accomplished every morning when the kids get ready for school. Why would you need me to tell you what to do?"

"But, Doris, I was just trying to be helpful. Why couldn't you simply tell me what needed to be done?"

"Because, Vic, I was already dealing with two children who couldn't figure things out for themselves. I don't need another child who can't solve problems independently. Having my partner act like one more person who can't potty without supervision was infuriating. I want someone that *I* can look to for help, not one more person that I have to guide through the basics."

"Why 'infuriating', Doris? Why is this such a big deal? It was just a lousy morning."

Doris stopped for a minute and considered why this thing with Vic got her so angry. It wasn't because it happened a lot, though that was true. And it wasn't because things were so hectic and pressured in the morning, though they were. She realized that when this kind of thing happened it made her feel both disappointed and anxious.

When Doris shared that with Vic, he was thoroughly confused.

"But, Doris, what's so anxiety provoking about morning, even a chaotic one?"

Doris realized that her reaction appeared out of proportion to the events. She tried to put it into words for Vic.

"It's not just about the small stuff that's going on at the time, Vic. It's that I feel let down when you're not taking initiative to solve the problem. I want you to be as responsible and capable as I am at figuring out what needs to be done and then doing it. That would feel like you're really my equal partner at those moments.

I think that the small stuff also serves as a basis for guessing about the big stuff. If you act dependent on me to do your thinking for you in a small crisis, how can I count on you to be a good partner in a big crisis? I want a partner who is competent, independent, and a problem-solver. If you look to me instead of thinking for yourself, then the only one *I* have to rely on is *myself.* That makes me angry and anxious. I suppose that it's both the disappointment and irritation of the moment on top of the anxiety that makes me react in such a big way to events that are in themselves so small."

Vic, understanding so much better what was going on for Doris, realized that he'd been relying on his partner to do the thinking for both of them in family situations. It was a habit born primarily of his own conviction that she knew so much better than he did what needed to be done. But he realized that it worked out to be an unfair burden on Doris.

He made a promise to himself, and to Doris, that he'd only ask Doris after he'd made a sincere effort to solve the problem for himself.

The day ended with hugs all around and a renewed closeness. It turned out to be a good day after all.

Vic's demonstration of his commitment to listening to Doris's point of view, and his persistence until he truly understood her feelings, persuaded Doris that he really wanted to be a good and equal partner to her. His responsiveness was clear in his promise to ask for Doris's input only after he'd attempted to solve the problem on his own. All of this contributed to Doris feeling both loved and secure. That after all was his real goal.

♥

Roles and responsibilities need to be negotiated so that
both parties feel considered and respected.

♥

Are you doing your share?

*T*heirs was a pretty conventional marriage in many ways. Nellie had primary responsibility for home and hearth. Randolph had the job that paid most of the bills. It was the way they had conceived of their marriage at the very beginning. It was just that now it wasn't quite as simple as they'd thought it would be. And neither was as satisfied with the division of responsibilities as they'd expected.

Nellie was overwhelmed with trying to carry full daily responsibility for the management of the house and kids. Today had been a pretty typical day. In the morning, the baby had to be taken to daycare; the 7 year old needed help taking in his show-and-tell project; and the 11 year old had to go to the orthodontist before school. During the school day, she'd gone into the school media center to help out with story times. For a few hours, she'd worked at her custom quilting business. After work, she'd picked up the dry-cleaning on the way to daycare, taken the 7 year old to Cub Scouts, and picked up the 11 year old from soccer. When she got home, she started cooking dinner and started running the first of 3 loads of laundry.

When Randolph got home from work, he sat down in the family room with his newspaper. He called to her from his chair and asked her when dinner would be ready. She found herself clenching her jaw as she answered. She was feeling very testy about his sitting down and relaxing while she was scurrying around trying to get everyone fed. Although she wasn't audible in the next room, she was muttering about how puzzling it was that a man who had so much education was apparently unable to learn how to assemble a salad, sauté vegetables, or cook pasta.

Randolph in the meantime was quietly worrying about the bills as he sat and looked at the newspaper. He knew that there'd been an orthodontist visit that day; he'd seen the bill for the new soccer cleats; and the monthly daycare bill was consistently chewing up the little discretionary money that he kept trying to set aside. He thought it was great that Nellie could be at the kids' school so much. It certainly made him feel secure knowing that she was so on top of the kids' educational experience. And he was delighted that she so enjoyed the quilting commissions that came her way.

Nellie called to him from the kitchen that she needed extra money in the checking account that month for the camping trip that the Cub Scouts would be taking. He found himself clenching his jaw as he yelled back that he'd take care of it. He was feeling pretty resentful that she could just speak and he'd be expected to spit out money like an ATM. How could a woman with a good education and a lot of practical skills feel that it wasn't her responsibility to help pay the bills for her family?

After dinner, and after the kids had been put to bed, they found themselves with a quiet hour. She let the rest of the laundry sit; he put aside the bills he was paying. And they talked. It was really tough not to just blame and be angry. But that evening there was magic – they talked, really talked, about what they each were feeling. He confessed that he was feeling overwhelmed by carrying almost all the financial responsibility for their family. She confessed that she felt resentful and exhausted from carrying almost all the household responsibility. Almost simultaneously they each asked, "Could you please consider helping me out?"

He offered to take over the cleaning and the grocery shopping plus all the Cub Scout and soccer responsibilities. She said that she could finish up her quilt commissions and look for a more lucrative job during school hours.

It wasn't the way they'd thought it would work when they were first starting out. It wasn't even the way they'd thought it <u>should</u> work. It just turned out to be the way that really <u>did</u> work. The roles and responsibilities turned out to be way less neat and defined. They found out that they needed more help than they'd expected, and that they were capable of giving way more than they'd expected to have to give. They each walked away from the moment feeling loved, supported, and respected. And that <u>was</u> what they'd hoped to feel in their marriage.

There is no one "right" way to divide up household roles and responsibilities. What defines rightness for any given relationship is that both parties feel that they've been considered and respected. If that part works, the details are negotiable.

♥

Men and women typically have different ideas about
the purpose of communication.

♥

What's the point?

Ken and Maria had been married only a year when the frustration set in. Ken had always prided himself on his ability at work to communicate the facts in the most efficient way possible. He was clear, concise, and organized. He was sure that his skill didn't desert him when he walked through the door to his home. The communication problem that was occurring between him and Maria was therefore very puzzling. She'd pose a question, he'd answer it, and she'd come back to him a little later with the same question posed in essentially the same way.

His frustration was mounting. She was neither deaf nor stupid, so the only explanation he could find for her behavior was that she was stubborn and manipulative.

Maria had her own frustration with the communication between them. When they'd been dating, the most magical thing was the way they could talk for endless hours, about everything and nothing. Now that they were married, they never just talked. Oh, they had conversational exchanges of information: "Can you take the dog to the vet?" or "Where do you want to go on vacation?" But they never just talked, where the purpose of the talking was simply being together in a particularly personal way. She felt like they were drifting apart, becoming cohabitants rather than partners.

She was really worried about the future of their relationship. She'd seen her own parents drift unhappily through a long marriage that seemed to have no intimacy. She was sure that its decline had started the same way, since her own father was never one to waste time or energy on "idle chatter".

Men and women typically have different ideas about the point of communication. In the masculine sphere, communication has as its purpose the sharing of information, the transmission of data from one person to another in order to complete a task. A secondary purpose is to establish the ownership of power– to have information is to be one-up, to need or seek information is to be one-down. (This is one reason some men hate to ask for directions.)

In the feminine sphere, communication has as its purpose the connection of people, the creation or sustenance of bonds. A secondary purpose is to share data. Women in fact will often generate questions in order to create a moment of connection. Not infrequently the posing of a question merely results in a statement of agreement from both parties ("Yes, I thought so."). The questions are the medium for connecting with another person. Just because there was no new information exchanged doesn't mean, for a woman, that the communication was fruitless. The connection was the fruit. In this kind of exchange, a man is more likely to wonder why the question was asked if the answer was already known.

It was in this sort of puzzle that Ken found himself with Maria. They described that the longer the conflict continued, the worse it was getting. They seemed to be bringing out the worst in each other. Ken's frustration and Maria's hurt feelings were increasing daily.

He angrily acknowledged that the more she repeated the questioning, the more abrupt his answers were becoming. He'd given her the data that she'd requested; why didn't she stop asking? He couldn't stand the whole pointless process and so was trying to make it as brief as possible. He found himself trying to avoid any conversation with her for fear that it would proceed in this pointless and unproductive way.

She tearfully said that the more abrupt he became, the more she felt compelled to drag some kind of engagement out of him. Since he didn't seem to have any interest in just talking, which to her meant an interest in connecting with her, all that she could think to do was ask him questions over and over. She was desperate to draw him toward her into an intimate connection. The more he withdrew, the more desperate she felt about the waning connection and so the more relentlessly she chased him.

As we talked about what was happening, it became clear that each of them was being driven in a counterproductive direction. But it also became clear that they wanted to be closer together. Neither of them was happy with the distance that was growing between them. They both wanted the communication to be successful, but neither of them had understood where the breakdown was occurring.

Maria came to realize that Ken wasn't trying to disconnect from her. She began to recognize that he was in fact completely open to hearing and responding to her wish for connection. He wanted to be connected to her. But he needed to hear in clear language a request for connection that wasn't in the form of a request for information. He was simply led in the wrong direction by her mode of approaching him. He heard a question, gave an answer, and thought that the communication had been completed successfully. It was therefore persistently frustrating to have the whole process repeat itself without any sign of progress at all.

Ken came to understand that Maria needed communication in order to feel connected. When she made her needs clear in language that he could make sense of, he could be responsive by intentionally participating in "just talking" time. He actually enjoyed "just talking" with her, as long as he was clear on what the purpose was. It was when he thought the purpose was something else that he got off track. At those times when he recognized that he was hearing the same question repeatedly, he knew to stop and deal not with the content of the question but with the underlying disconnection that she was feeling between them. He had never meant to disconnect. She had not understood that it was just his way of addressing what he thought was an information exchange.

As they both moved to a place of greater understanding about the nature of the differences between masculine and feminine communication, it became easier to use communication to bring them closer together rather than to drive them apart.

♥

It's easy to get caught up in primitive
behaviors of self-defense.

♥

Fight or flight is NOT a plan

*I*magine that we ran an experiment together. First, I injected you with a mix of all of the chemicals your body naturally produces when you are under any kind of stress, whether it's a near miss on the highway or a fight with a store clerk or a wolf at your campsite. Next, we wait a moment for the chemicals to take effect, which happens very rapidly. Now you're feeling this chemical cascade—your pulse is rapid, your breathing shallow. You can't tell offhand, but your circulation is also being diverted to your internal organs and your digestion has been put on hold. Also, your brain is working differently, with attention diffuse and scattered in a way that's good for noticing quickly if an enemy approaches. Okay, you're ready— now discuss with your partner all the most sensitive issues about your relationship. And do it with sensitivity, patience, and focused attention. Do it without defensiveness, even though your body and brain are chemically prepared primarily for defense.

Sounds like a lousy plan, doesn't it? You don't need to be a psychologist to predict that the outcome of this kind of set-up will be poor. No one can be expected to perform well at these higher level human tasks when his or her physiology is organized for the completely different and extremely primitive challenges of fight or flight. Biological preparation that was good for fleeing from saber-toothed tigers and is still good for running the mile is terrible for doing your taxes or working out relationship issues with your partner.

Psychologists demonstrated a long time ago that there is an optimal level of emotional and physical arousal for performance of challenging tasks. Less arousal than this and you really don't put out your best effort. More arousal than this and you can't.

When couples get into fights or heated exchanges, it can happen quickly that arousal escalates for either or both partner(s). Before you know it, you're right in the middle of our experiment and expecting to perform well at a very difficult and demanding task. It's easy to get caught up in pretty primitive behaviors of self-defense or even attack – behaviors that anyone in his or her right mind would recognize immediately as counterproductive. But of course, you're not in your right mind; you're in your chemically altered mind.

There is a solution. Everybody can have at his or her disposal a collection of techniques that are effective for reducing the arousal. These relaxation or self-soothing techniques are easy to learn, easy to practice, even easy to implement at difficult moments. Psychologist John Gottman teaches couples in his "Love Lab" at University of Washington a program of these techniques as part of their work with his team. But you don't need to have formal instruction to learn or use these strategies. They require no equipment; they're free and easy and always accessible to you.

There are 2 key techniques, sometimes to be used together, sometimes as alternatives. The first is the strategic use of separation – when things get intense, the partners separate while things settle down. Two rules – the first is that the separation should last for 20 minutes. There is a subtle biorhythm that uses a 20 minute repair cycle. Most of what you need to have happen to get you out of our doomed experiment and into a better emotional and biologic place will occur within those 20 minutes. Less than 20 minutes and you're not quite squared away physiologically; more than 20 minutes is usually unnecessary and can be counterproductive.

The second rule is that during the separation, partners are not to think about the argument or the issues. Thoughts should be neutral. Take a walk and focus on the scenery, read a magazine, or do something comparable, purposefully diverting yourself from the subject of the fight or your partner, thus allowing your body to settle down.

The second key strategy is to use a relaxation technique. The simplest and most universally effective is the slow, deep exhale. This simple form of breathing modification effectively slows and then halts the chemical cascade of fight or flight. The technique is the essence of simplicity – breathe out through gently pursed lips (do not blow); breathe out as slowly as you can, counting to at least 6; breathe out as deeply as you can, until you have emptied as much air as you comfortably can. Repeat as often as you need. This technique can be used anywhere at any time, including during an intense discussion with your partner. If you can utilize this technique early enough in the arousal cycle, you may not need to move to separation. The general guideline is that if you can keep your heart rate below 100 beats per minute you can perform the higher level tasks adequately.

We are all essentially chemically driven creatures. We have the knowledge and capacity to manage our chemistry or we can be managed by it. But there's no percentage in ignoring it. It's going to happen with or without your willing participation.

In Gottman's Love Lab, he has couples wear pulse monitors to alert them when their heart rates are indicating that they are too physiologically aroused to function well and cooperatively.

You can train yourself to recognize when you are operating at "fight or flight" level instead of collaboratively. No matter how justified you may feel your arousal is, it will not serve you well as part of an intimate interpersonal communication.

Do yourself and your relationship a favor—cool it, with one technique or another. Re-enter the communication arena when you are truly in charge of your body and your mind.

♥

Sometimes an accusation is really a question in disguise.

♥

When an accusation is really a question

"You really want a 19 year old blonde, not me!"
"I know you're just waiting for the right moment to leave me!"

*I*t's possible, of course, that either of these statements could be true, a simple statement of fact. It's also true that either of these accusations might instead represent a question in disguise.

Kristin is 47 years old and brunette. She's thoroughly aware that this culture reveres youth and defines blondes as more attractive than brunettes. Her fear is that her husband of 24 years is no longer satisfied with her. Her message is framed as an accusation. The accusation covers up her anxiety under cover of anger. The real message is a question: "Do you still want to be married to me, even though I'm neither 19 nor blonde?"

If her husband, Mel, simply defends himself against the accusation – "No, I don't." – he's missed the point. A denial of the charge is not by itself enough to make Kristin feel secure in his affection. She needs him to answer the question that she was afraid to ask. Instead of denial he could answer the unasked questions: does he love her more than the day he married her? is she beautiful to him? does he want to stay married to her forever? Then he's taken a step toward effectively addressing her anxiety. If he settles for denial, then the unanswered question will resurface over and over. In fact, since the anxiety wasn't adequately addressed, it's likely that the anxiety will increase. The accusations may escalate, not because Mel's done something new to earn her wrath but because he's failed to assuage her anxiety. She's been left to stew in her own worry. This in itself is painful and will make her angry.

People in relationships frequently complain that they're being accused of things of which they aren't guilty. It's not crazy to be angry at being accused unjustly. It's also not crazy to defend yourself when you feel attacked. It is, however, more practical to respond to the accusations in a way that leads to a good result between partners. Sometimes the most productive course involves answering questions that may not even have been asked rather than denying accusations that have been shouted.

Let's look at the second example. Marietta and Ken have been married for two years. Ken is devoted to Marietta but is unsure whether she feels the same way about him. He's very affectionate and she's rather reserved. He's likely to engage in all sorts of spontaneous gestures of affection. She won't even initiate a hug. Since her natural behavior is so different from his, he finds himself misinterpreting hers regularly. Over the course of two years, he's come to wonder whether her lack of spontaneous gestures of affection in fact represents a lack of love.

One evening, when Marietta was describing a friend's recent divorce, Ken's anxiety flared. It was then that he accused her of being ready to leave him. Marietta was in fact thoroughly committed to Ken. She was not only stunned by his statement, she was hurt. That she enjoyed receiving his affection was a powerful testament to her love for him. To be accused so unjustly enraged her. Her impulse was first to deny the accusation and then to accuse him of being an insensitive pig. Instead she withheld her righteous anger and tried to figure out what the disguised question might be.

The easiest place to start is with the accusation itself. Is there a way to turn it around to become the question? For Marietta, the question she tried out in her mind was, "Is Ken worried that I'm looking for the right moment to leave him?" That seemed to match the accusation, so she responded to the question instead of the accusation. She told Ken that she was deeply committed to him and to their marriage, that she loved him with all her heart and that she hoped to celebrate their 50th anniversary together.

By responding to the unasked question, a partner can attend to the underlying feelings and concerns. By doing this the relationship is nurtured and sustained. The outcome then is positive and constructive and moves the relationship ahead. Just because an accusation has been made doesn't mean that either a denial or a defense must be offered. Sometimes responding to what your partner hasn't said– might even be afraid to say– can be the best way for a conversation to go.

♥

Both partners in a relationship require and deserve
to have their needs met.

♥

I can't do that; but I can do this

Sylvia had stayed home from work all day with two sick children. She was exhausted and desperate for adult contact. She'd been watching the clock, counting the minutes until Greg would arrive home from work.

Greg was counting the miles home, eager for the peaceful retreat into his "castle". It had been a particularly unpleasant day at work and he couldn't wait to be home.

When Greg walked through the door, he felt all the muscles in his back relax as he went off-duty. Sylvia felt her own mood lighten immediately when another adult arrived and she could go off-duty. As soon as Greg walked in, she handed him the baby and launched into a litany of what she'd been through all day. Greg felt every muscle re-tighten and a powerful urge to flee. He handed back the baby, mumbled something, and retreated to the bathroom with the newspaper and stayed there for an hour. By the time he reappeared, Sylvia was livid, alternating between crying and cursing.

Greg felt assaulted and Sylvia felt abandoned. They were in agreement about attending therapy, because each believed that it would be a chance to get an objective observer to agree with the obvious justness of their own feelings. They were surprised to find out that as the therapist I believed that both positions were just and legitimate. We discussed a more satisfactory way of resolving such impasses that's founded on the principle that both partners in a relationship require and deserve to have their basic needs met.

I've described before the importance in communication of listening, understanding, and responding. I'm going to focus here on <u>responding</u>. Responding is defined as a change in behavior based on listening and understanding. Responding isn't obedience. It doesn't imply "doing what you're told". It does imply that your behavior is influenced by receiving and processing your partner's communications. It's possible that your partner may ask something of you that you don't feel that you can give. You can still be responsive without complying exactly with the request.

In the above example, Sylvia wanted an immediate opportunity to share her day and have Greg participate by listening, sympathizing, and supporting her. Greg came home feeling completely tapped out. He didn't feel that he could at that moment do and be what Sylvia needed. He wanted peace and quiet. As it turned out, neither got what they needed, so it was a lose-lose outcome.

Imagine how a win-win might have looked instead, after they'd learned new problem-solving strategies. Imagine that Greg had come home, heard Sylvia begin her story, and realized the nature of her day and the immediacy of her need. But he also knew the nature of his day and the immediacy of his own needs. From a win-win perspective, he knew that a good outcome would respect both people's needs.

In this revised scenario, rather than flee, Greg kept the baby in his arms while he said, "Syl, I can see that you've had a horrible day and really need me to be there for you. And I want to do that for you. But I've also had a killer day and I'm running on empty. Before I can be there for you, I need to recharge my own batteries. How about half an hour to change my clothes and check the newspaper headlines, and then I'll be able to be there for you the way that you need?"

Greg isn't asking permission; he's asking if this format is workable for Sylvia as a compromise that responds to her needs and respects his needs as well. ("I can't do that [listen right now], but I can do this [listen in half an hour].") If it's workable, then she'll accept it as offered. If it's not, then she can offer a counter-plan that better meets her needs while still responding to what Greg has told her about his own needs.

Although Sylvia would prefer to have his immediate attention, she hears his fatigue. Because he's been responsive and has made a sincere statement of commitment to meet her needs, she can delay actually getting her needs met for a little while. *As long as a partner believes that the other is being responsive, then it becomes possible to compromise.* With responsiveness comes trust that your partner has a commitment to meet your needs, even if it can't be immediately.

Sylvia might have come back with a counter offer that felt more manageable for her,

"Okay, I hear your exhaustion too. How about 20 minutes?"

Greg, feeling that Sylvia was being responsive to him, was able to compromise and come back adequately, if not completely, refreshed after 20 minutes of time to himself

Responsiveness leads to trust. Trust gives you the flexibility to compromise. Compromise permits partners to create those lovely win-win outcomes.

♥

We all crave the experience of feeling known, understood, and accepted
by our partners.

♥

Acceptance is the highest form of love

We all crave the experience of feeling fully known and under-stood by our partners. Having someone want to know you is very powerful stuff. More potent still is the feeling that your partner knows you, with all your endearing and irritating traits, and loves you.

Elizabeth was fussing over the packing details – was there enough shampoo for the whole trip? Did she have a warm enough sweater if the weather turned cool? Would there be room for the souvenirs or should she take an extra tote? The list of things to worry about went on and on.

Doug, who'd finished packing for himself hours ago, wandered into the bedroom and found her pulling on her hair, as she always did when stressed.

"Lizzie, how's it going?"

She shared her litany of concerns, he shared his opinions when asked (plenty of shampoo, take an extra jacket, he had room for souvenirs, etc.), and he wandered back downstairs to watch TV. As he sat down on the couch, his son, Mark, laughed and said, "I bet Mom's having her usual packing meltdown. Doesn't it make you crazy? Why don't you tell her to chill?"

Doug smiled at Mark and shrugged. "Look, I don't fuss the way your mom does, but it's her way. It doesn't cost me anything when she does this – she doesn't make me stay and fuss with her. It's just how she handles the stresses of traveling. I admit that I don't see the point exactly, but so what? It's her way."

"Dad," Mark said, with the wisdom of all of his 14 years, "she's worrying about nothing. It seems stupid. Why not just explain to her why it's dumb?"

Doug laughed. "First of all, she doesn't agree that it's dumb. She thinks it's 'thorough'. Secondly, it wouldn't change anything. She'd feel just as anxious; she'd just feel she had to hide it from me. Part of loving someone is helping them to feel that they can be who they are with you. I love your mom. I don't need her to do everything my way for me to love her. I actually find this nuttiness endearing."

"You *like* when Mom acts like a nutcase?"

"Mark, your mom is smart and competent 98% of the time. This is just one of her most human traits. It's no big deal when she has these bonkers moments. It's harmless; cut her some slack. Besides, you have your own human moments. Don't you like it when the people who love you accept them, and accept you?"

Mark bristled. "Like what?"

"Like when you have to stop at every store window on Main Street to look at your reflection and check your hair. Like having to eat macaroni and cheese for luck before every basketball game."

"Well,..."

"See? We could explain to you that it's 'dumb', or we can just accept it as part of you. We love you, it's harmless, so we accept it. It's the loving thing to do."

Elizabeth walked into the family room in time to hear the last part of the conversation. She walked over to them, ruffled Mark's hair as she passed, and gave Doug a hug.

"So, sweetheart, when are we leaving for the airport in the morning?"

"The flight's at 8, so I figure we're good if we get there at 5. I'll set the alarm for 3:30."

"Dear, you know we only have to be there <u>two</u> hours early and it only takes 20 minutes to get to the airport."

"Nonsense, Lizzie; you just never know about traffic or about airports."

"Yes, dear. Three hours it is."

And she turned and winked at Mark as she kissed Doug on the head and then walked quietly away, smiling.

Whether your partner finds your habits endearing or irritating, it is a powerful demonstration of love to experience your partner's acceptance of you. Each person is a package deal—some good stuff, some not so good stuff. When you feel that your partner truly sees you for who you are, sees the best and the worst of you, and loves the whole you, that's to feel loved and secure in the relationship. When that love is expressed in demonstrations of acceptance, that is one potent demonstration of responsiveness.

♥

If what you're doing now isn't working for you, change it.

♥

Applying principles of cognitive therapy

*O*ne of the critical achievements in human cognitive develop-ment is the ability to think about your own thinking. One of the critical achievements in theories of psychotherapy is the recognition that, since you can think about your thinking, it may be possible to CHANGE your thinking.

Cognitive Behavioral Therapy (CBT), Rational Emotive Behavioral Therapy (REBT), and Positive Psychology are all founded on the principle that you can willfully change the way you think. And that when you change the way you think, you change the way you feel. Changing the way you behave can both precede and follow changing the way you think.

If the way you're thinking about something (or everything) isn't working for you, change it. By "working for you", I mean, is it getting you the results that you want? Is it making you happy? Is it making you successful in your interactions with other people?

Much of what is experienced is founded not only on the objective nature of events, but also on how you think about those events. For example, winning $5 in the lottery would, objectively, be considered a good thing. If you had your heart set on winning 10 million dollars, if you felt that you needed that 10 million dollars to be happy or safe or successful, then winning $5 could be a crushing disappointment. <u>What</u> happens and how you feel about it can be very different things.

With a partner, the objective nature of an event can be thoroughly obscured by the perception of that event. For example, a partner who asks how you feel might be perceived, objectively, as a good partner. If you were hoping, expecting, or needing that partner to be intuitive enough to know how you feel without asking, the experience of being asked could be very disappointing.

However, it is possible willfully to change how you look at the experience. If you choose to focus on your partner's intentions, you may be able to recognize the inherent positive aspect of the event. If you recognize that your expectations might have been unrealistic, you may be able to recalibrate and more highly value what you <u>did</u> receive and be less disappointed by what you didn't.

Although we often feel as if our experiences just happen to us, in fact they are highly processed cognitive events; and we're the ones processing them. We are much more capable than we often recognize of willfully managing our cognitive experiences.

If what you're doing now isn't working for you, change it. If the way you think about things leaves you unhappy, disappointed, scared, or angry, consider that you have the power to change all that by having the power to change how you think. If you change the way you think, your feelings and your behavior can change as well. You don't have to be the victim of experience. What you do with that experience is up to you. You may need help to recognize or utilize your power for change; but the power is already within you.

♥

As a relationship ages, it becomes easy to
notice the bad and overlook the good.

♥

Catch your partner doing well

When a relationship is new, it's easy to notice the good things. As the relationship ages, it becomes increasingly easy to notice the bad and overlook the good.

When Frank and Babette first got together it was an unending exchange of pleasant surprises. They were so acutely aware every time one of them did something positive. Each positive thing was a delight to observe and a pleasure to comment on. The first time Babette saw Frank spontaneously rinse out his dishes and put them in the dishwasher, she got a warm glow inside from this demonstration of domestic behavior and went over and wrapped her arms around him and kissed him on the cheek. When Frank saw Babette sit down to balance her checkbook at the end of the month, he admired her fiscal responsibility and picked her up and swung her around in his arms before putting her down with a kiss on her nose.

The first time he put his shoes away before going to bed; the first time she put away all of her tools at the end of a project; the first time he brought her tea when he saw her come home all droopy from a tough day at work; the first time she picked up his dry-cleaning because she knew he might not have time – each positive behavior noticed and commented on. Each of them felt appreciated and encouraged. They came to expect good things from each other.

As the relationship matured, they came to take the good things for granted. Worse, they became more and more aware of the negative things.Babette was used to Frank picking up fresh bagels for Sunday brunch. She'd long ago stopped thanking him for this loving gesture. This time, when he forgot the blueberry bagel for which she'd recently developed a fondness, she huffed at him about his thoughtlessness. Frank, ignoring the fact that Babette had put out his favorite cream cheese, as she always did, snapped that he'd forgotten because he had had to stop and get gas because she'd let the gas tank get too low.

So here was a situation where two partners had taken a fundamentally positive and loving event and twisted it into a fight. Each was quick to recognize a (minor) failure on their partner's part. Each was failing to notice the positive and loving gesture that was happening right in front of their eyes.

> *Here's the progression—*
>
> The more positive behaviors we receive from our partners → the more we become accustomed to them.
>
> The more accustomed we become → the easier it is to take the positive for granted and to fail to notice it.
>
> The less we notice the positive → the easier it is to notice the negative.
>
> The more we notice the negative → the more the negative comes to define our image of our partners.
>
> The more negative our images of our partners → the less we want to do positive things for our partners.

It's a nasty little cycle. Perversely, it is most likely to happen to couples where there has been a lot of positive behavior in the early stages of the relationship. It took the positive behaviors becoming regular and familiar to launch the cycle. If positive behaviors were rare, they would remain remarkable. The less kind your partner, the more you would value each rarely committed kindness. So only the good guys suffer here. Not fair, but true.

But as common as the cycle is, it can be broken. It starts with a willful change in consciousness. It may have become an unconscious habit to notice every time your partner did something wrong or imperfectly. It can become a conscious habit to notice every time your partner does something right.

Babette can re-train herself to pay attention to the fact that Frank went out early Sunday to get those bagels. She can express her appreciation for those fresh, warm bagels and choose not to mention the absence of the blueberry ones, simply reminding him before his next bagel run.

Frank can comment on the pleasure of always finding his favorite cream cheese on the brunch table and refrain from commenting on the half empty gas tank until another time. Enjoying the experience both of brunch and of feeling appreciated transmutes the experience back into a loving one.

Catch your partner doing well. The positive will come back to you many times over. The progression becomes this—

Looking for the positive → noticing what's good about your partner.

Noticing the good → reacquainting yourself with why you were attracted to this person in the first place.

Being reminded of the initial attraction → noticing the negative things less.

Noticing the negative less → increased appreciation of your partner.

Increased appreciation → it becoming easier to notice the positive.

The more you notice the positive things about your partner → the more you enjoy being with your partner and the better your partner feels about being with you.

It is a self-perpetuating POSITIVE cycle. It's a matter of conscious intention and choice. Just as noticing the negative had become a habit, now noticing the positive can become a habit as well.

♥

A balance of judging our partners by
BOTH their efforts and the outcome.

♥

The best of intentions

*H*ow are we to judge our partners—by their efforts or by the outcome?

Marcus left the office early so that he could stop on the way home and pick up Danita's dry-cleaning for tonight's fundraiser. He knew that she was hoping to wear that particular dress tonight. As he stepped off the elevator at work, he bumped into his boss, who grabbed him for a quick discussion of the presentation they were giving to a big client the next day. As he glanced at his watch, he was relieved to see that he still had just enough time to get to the cleaners before heading home. As he started the car, he noticed that he had let the gas tank get close to empty. The last time they'd run out of gas, Danita had threatened to dismember him if it ever happened again, so he made a beeline to the nearest gas station. Okay, no time for the cleaners, but he'd still get home on schedule. By this time, he was just in time to catch the rush hour crush, so the trip home took about 25% longer than he'd figured. As he dashed in the door, 15 minutes late, with no dress in hand, Danita glared at him, said, "That is so like you," and turned away to finish getting ready.

Marcus ran through the gamut of emotions. First he felt really bad – sad and guilty, because he'd arrived late and without her dress. Then he felt really defensive – after all, he'd really tried. Then he was just angry – he was getting no credit for all his thoughtfulness and even having put aside his own work in order to take care of her needs. By the time they were driving to the fundraiser together, they were both seething. She was furious that he once again was late and hadn't brought her dress; he was furious that he was getting no credit for his efforts.

From his point of view, he was being judged totally on results without consideration of intentions. She should know that he'd really tried but just couldn't make it work. He expected her to see past the poor results and be able to intuit the good intentions.

From her point of view, he was always saying that he'd <u>tried</u>, but it so often turned out to be that he had little or nothing to show for his efforts. She could see the results and they were not good. His intentions were not apparent to her; but she believed that sincerely good intentions would be apparent in good results.

Truthfully, she found it all confusing and frustrating. She believed him to be a good person; but she couldn't reconcile that image with the man who so often disappointed her. She was beginning to feel foolish when she expected a positive outcome. "Proof's in the pudding", her grandmother had always said.

The next day, Marcus arrived at work in pretty irritable condition. On top of last night's fiasco with Danita, he had the anxiety about today's presentation to the important client. He called the workgroup together to finalize details for the meeting. The junior member of the team, Lee, immediately blurted out that he didn't have the glossy brochures they'd worked up for the client. He started to explain that the IT department had had a major crash, Super Office Works had promised the job for yesterday but been delayed, his car was in the shop so he couldn't go get the brochures that were now sitting ready at the printer's, ... Marcus stopped him and said coldly, "Am I supposed to take these excuses to the client instead of the brochures? It's results that count, kid."

Later that day, Marcus was working on an evaluation of the workgroup's performance. He was really struggling with what to do about Lee. He knew that Lee was very committed to his work and often did a good job. But sometimes he messed up – he didn't show adequate forethought, undertook too much work, or just got overwhelmed. Sometimes he just didn't seem to allow any leeway for the unpredictable things that would inevitably happen on a project to slow it down. How was Marcus to judge him – on his results, which were at best mixed; or on his intentions, which seemed sincere? Was this one of those situations where it was an "A" for effort? That kind of grading had expired in kindergarten.

Despite his sympathy for Lee, it was the bottom line of the evaluation form that stopped him in his tracks. It said, "Would you choose to have this person on your team again?" Would he choose to work again with someone whose intentions were good but whose performance wasn't something he could count on?

Marcus suddenly flashed on his fight with Danita. Was this what she was struggling with too? It seemed to Marcus that he was feeling the need to judge Lee only on results while he was insisting that Danita judge him only on intentions.

He closed Lee's evaluation with the comment that he was "aware of and respected Lee's commitment to his work but that future work assignments should be dependent on evidence of improved performance."

After he'd submitted Lee's evaluation, Marcus sat and puzzled over the question of intentions vs. outcomes. He hoped that Danita could recognize his commitment to her, just as he recognized Lee's commitment to his work. He felt both his and Lee's commitments to be sincere.

But even with a sincere commitment, he didn't feel that he could consistently rely on Lee. There were always legitimate sounding explanations for why the outcome wasn't what was promised or what was needed. He had to admit, as he had on Lee's evaluation, that Lee's bottom-line just wasn't good enough for Marcus to want to work with him on anything that really mattered.

Being honest with himself, he had to admit that sometimes he let himself get sloppy with his obligations to Danita. He really didn't always leave time for the circumstances that he had reason to anticipate. He often took on more obligations than he could possibly expect to complete successfully. He nodded as he admitted, only to himself, that he often hoped that he'd get away with good intentions without delivering on his promises. Also to himself, he argued too that sometimes it really wasn't his fault! At those times he was hoping that Danita would be willing to look past the failed outcome and judge him instead on his sincerely good intentions.

Perhaps the best approach then is to come to some kind of balance of judging our partners by BOTH their efforts and the outcome. It is important to give credit for intention, when it's honest and sincere. It is also important to recognize the impact of the outcomes. Neither exists without the reality of the other, and both matter.

If you're hoping that your partner will judge you exclusively on intentions, you're not being fair or realistic. If you're not giving your partner any credit for good intentions, you're not being kind.

♥

Our expectations play a big role in our satisfaction.

♥

Every moment is not bliss

*O*ur expectations play a big role in our satisfaction. Sometimes, our beliefs about how things should be can lead us to unnecessary anxiety or disappointment.

Sue was listening to her twenty-something daughter, Eliza, waxing poetic about her fiancé, Miguel. There were stories about laughter shared, about romantic dinners by candlelight, about walks through the woods.

It was wonderful stuff; and Sue remembered having just such moments with her husband of 24 years, Norman. She was thrilled for Eliza, and was enjoying every moment of listening to her and watching the stars in her eyes.

She was also wondering if and how to tell Eliza that marriage wasn't really much like courtship.

She was wondering about telling Eliza about the parts of marriage that were not so blissful. She was remembering the first time she had the flu and vomited all over the bed, with Norman in it. Or the time that Norman had a kidney stone and the sound of the scream when he passed it.

She was remembering the first time she was up all night with a teething baby and the really nasty things she said to Norman the next day. She was remembering the really ugly things he said to her after he lost the promotion because she begged him not to move the family to Mississippi.

There were wonderful times too, of course; and Eliza had certainly seen those. She'd seen innumerable hugs and kisses between her parents, lots of laughter, and being there for each other during the challenges of illness, relocations, and loss.

But it was essentially invisible when Sue and Norman weren't intimate for three months because of Norman's flirting. It was not obvious when, on any given day, one of them wasn't much liking the other, for whatever reason.

And Eliza wouldn't have been present when Sue had spoken with loathing of Norman's brother, who was constantly asking for a "loan". Nor would she have been there when Norman hissed that Sue's mom was a tyrant whose "heart condition" was all in her head.

It wasn't that Sue wanted to take anything away from Eliza's happiness or from her blissful anticipation of her marriage to Miguel. Sue liked Miguel and fully expected him to make an excellent husband.

But Sue was worried that Eliza's naïve expectations might lead her to doubt her relationship with Miguel as soon as things got ugly, or messy, or nasty. She was worried that Eliza might be so disappointed by the disorderly realities of marriage (and life) that she'd believe that she'd made a mistake by marrying Miguel. She worried that Eliza would blame life's dissatisfactions on some inherent flaw in the marriage. Rather she wanted her to see that marriage is more like an epic poem than either a limerick or a sonnet.

After much reflection, Sue decided that there was little value in having that conversation with Eliza while she was in a state of premarital bliss. She made a mental note, though, to talk about such things when the opportunities arose after the wedding. Sue wanted Eliza's marriage to be both happy and long.

Sometimes an expectation that things will be flawless, easy, and spontaneously perfect can backfire horribly. When the reality doesn't match the fantasy, it can be easy to believe, erroneously, that the reality is defective, and that it should be replaced. With relationships in particular, it's important to understand that even the best marriages aren't perfect and that they rarely start out as the best marriages.

♥

We can increase marital satisfaction by improving
the realistic nature of our expectations.

♥

Expectations

*M*y cell phone won't work in the grocery store or in elevators. The touchpad on my laptop sometimes refuses to acknowledge my existence. My car needs to go in to Service to repair the air conditioner that needed also to be repaired last summer.

There are days when I just throw my hands up in disgust and curse technology.

Of course, I'm only cursing it because I depend on it. I depend on it because it is so valuable in my life. So when it fails me, even momentarily, I get angry and resentful.

I get angry and resentful because I expect it to work ALL the time, seamlessly, never letting me down, always there when I need it. Isn't that what technology's for, after all?

I could become a reactionary and reject all technology. I could say that if it's not going to behave perfectly then I'm not going to rely on it at all. I could say that if it's not going to be perfect always then I'm not going to use it ever.

I could indulge my nostalgia and say things like, "No one ever lost the data on a paper calendar because of a 'virus'." Or, "Nobody ever lost an hour's writing because a legal tablet 'crashed' during a power failure."

Then the nostalgia fades and is replaced with thoughts like, "But my cell phone beeps to alert me to appointments. And it lets me carry a calculator, a mini-computer, address book, calendar, novel, and games, as well as access my patient data, all in one tidy and tiny package that works well ALMOST all of the time."

I don't even want to remember trying to do extensive word-processing without a PC. The memories bring shudders of horror.

Where does this leave me? Practically speaking, it leaves me once more embracing the technology that I have, grateful for what it does do and how often it does it well, recognizing that I have to accept that it will not perform perfectly all the time, no matter how annoyed I get at the failures. When I encounter a piece of technology that is intolerably unreliable, I first try to repair it. If that is unsuccessful or too costly, then I must part with it and move on.

The BBC News recently reported on an article in the <u>Journal of Personality and Social Psychology</u> in which the subject of expectations was investigated. In this report, it was suggested that many newlyweds suffer from unrealistic expectations that their new partners will be essentially perfect spouses. It was further suggested that these unmet expectations were to blame for the failure of so many marriages.

Interestingly, even people who have come to expect a certain frequency of failure in the technology in their lives still expect the partner in their lives to function without error or malfunction. Microsoft has to take a lot of credit for successfully training us to accept regular crashes of our PCs. We curse and then we reboot. We learn to save data regularly and to make backup disks in anticipation of the computer's sudden failure to perform adequately. We're not happy about the failures, but we accept them as an unavoidable part of computer use. We grumble, we correct, and we move forward with our work, mostly not missing much of a beat at all.

Can we learn from our own resilience? Can we come to think of our partners with the same attitude of tolerance that we extend to our technology?

For most of us, a serious relationship is significantly more romantic than the ownership of a new computer, cell phone, or car. That romance can blind us to the reality that our expectations of our new partner may be unfair and unrealistic. We may carry around the belief, at least initially, that the new romantic partner is near perfect. If something happens to damage that illusion, we may move forward nonetheless, but sometimes with the unrealistic expectation that the moment of failure was a unique event, never to recur or never to be joined in history by another, different failure. Then, when that illusion is destroyed by further evidence of imperfect function, some of us jump to the conclusion that this "unit"/partner needs to be replaced.

If expectations determine satisfaction, then we can increase the rate of marital satisfaction by improving the nature of our expectations. I'm not suggesting that expectations be eliminated or reduced to the ridiculous. But perhaps they can be made more realistic. Shouldn't love mean that we tolerate our partners even more than we tolerate our computers?

♥

Your partner should come to the relationship with
a commitment to find out what your
needs are and to meet them.

♥

Is it a fatal flaw?

And they lived happily ever after . . .

A romantic fantasy in our culture is that once you've met the "right" person, that person will *intuitively* understand how to meet your needs and will invariably demonstrate a capacity to know what it is that you need AND how to meet that need.

It's a short leap to believing, or fearing, that a failure by your partner to meet your need spontaneously, accurately, and perfectly might indicate that this person is not in fact the "right" person. It's this kind of thinking that can lead to that dreaded exchange:

"What do you want me to do?"

"If you really loved me, you'd already know."

Let me try to make a case for a different reality. In this one, your partner comes into the situation without knowledge of your needs. In this reality, there's no expectation that your partner has any extensive understanding of how you think or feel. Instead, your partner comes to the relationship with a deep and abiding commitment to find out what your needs are and to meet them. No more, no less. The slate is clean and the motives pure.

There's an implication here of shared responsibility. If your partner arrives without foreknowledge or capacity to mind-read, then the only way to obtain the information about your needs is from you. You have someone standing in front of you with a clearly stated wish to please you. But this person has no magical intuitive understanding of what to do for you. What are you going to do with this person? Are you going to say, "If you don't know, I won't tell you"? It does sound a bit childish. Yet it's what we sometimes do to our partners. We disregard their willingness to meet our needs and focus on the failure to perform guesswork successfully.

Although the traditional fantasy is supported by the magical ability to guess well, the reality is supported by the more realistic willingness to learn. In the fantasy, the "right" partner understands you like no one else ever has and then acts to meet your needs before you can even express them. In reality, the "right" partner is the one who may start out clueless about your needs but is committed to learning about them and then acting to meet them.

A parallel situation is when you discover that your partner may not spontaneously want exactly what you want. For example, you may have a powerful wish to have children. Your partner might actively prefer not to have kids. Is this a fatal flaw in the relationship? Well, it might be. It depends on how invested in the divergent positions <u>both</u> parties are.

In the traditional fantasy, rightness is defined as both parties agreeing consistently from the outset. In the reality, what matters isn't the match or mismatch of the *original* positions. It's the ability and willingness of the partners to move from the original positions to a place of better match. If your partner says, "I can and will modify my position in order to nurture this relationship", then you've received a powerful statement of love and commitment.

In the course of a long term relationship, it's this willingness and ability to shift position with a clear view of the bigger picture that will enable the partners to grow and develop *together.* A partner's ability to intuit your wishes and needs is a pleasant fantasy. It is however a partner's willingness to be responsive to your wishes and needs that will be meaningful and gratifying over time.

Men and women grow up in such different sub-cultures that they really don't arrive at a relationship with any substantial understanding of the other gender's experience. Those moments when your partner does demonstrate a clear and spontaneous understanding of your feelings need to be treated as gifts. If you begin to think of them instead as entry requirements, you're likely to be repeatedly disappointed.

A divergence of thinking isn't necessarily a case of having chosen the "wrong" partner or of recognizing a fatal flaw in the relationship. It could simply represent the natural course of things between two people of different backgrounds. Look for your partner's willingness to learn and to be responsive; value that. Those things will ultimately serve you better than any fantasy.

♥

Even in the absence of certainty,
you choose to proceed as if you were certain.

♥

Choosing trust

*I*n the third Indiana Jones movie, <u>The Last Crusade</u>, Jones is faced with a crisis – his father has been mortally wounded and the only way to save him is for Jones to face (and defeat) the lethal trials that guard the path to the Holy Grail. Each potentially fatal barrier to his passage is a test of his knowledge and his faith. The final challenge on the path is the necessity of crossing a bottomless chasm. It's obvious that there's no way across. Yet it's certain that to turn back is to watch his father die. This is a test of his willingness to make a leap of faith.

Faced with what appears to be clear visual evidence that the crossing cannot be made, can he find sufficient faith to proceed nonetheless? We have the opportunity to observe Jones's struggle: to turn back is certain defeat and loss; to proceed is to risk his life and limb without any guarantee of success. As Jones finds the will to move forward, we see his determination and his terror. A rock bridge has been hidden from his view by an optical illusion in the chamber. It's only by committing himself to move forward that he finds it. Because he chooses to make the leap of faith, he's able to continue on the path that can lead to success and the chance to save his father's life.

Although few of us will lead lives of such adventure as Indiana Jones, all of us are faced with such tests of faith. Not all of these tests are of a religious nature or of life or death dimension. A great many of them happen in the course of common interactions with the people in our lives.

Each day thousands of people stand in front of some official person and take marriage vows, swearing to stay married "'til death do us part". Each couple is committing itself to its own crusade. A great many of these couples will find themselves faced with a dilemma similar to Indiana Jones's. At some point in the marriage, there will be a crisis – to proceed is to move forward without any certainty of success but with great risk of pain. To give up is to face certain loss. Which way do you leap?

To a degree, this is a personality question. Some people will simply choose certainty over uncertainty, even if that certainty is of failure or loss. But the choice has practical considerations, not just for one given crisis but for overall risk management in relationships. You're choosing a lifestyle. Trust is a particular way of moving through life, with its own rhythms and directions. Distrust requires certain maintenance activities, like checking up on people, monitoring their activities.

To choose to trust is to move through your life choosing faith while knowing that at some point the rock bridge may not be there. To choose trust is to know that you may fall sometime but choosing to walk there anyway because that's where the beauty, truth, or love will be found. To choose trust is saying that it's gratifying to be part of a relationship built around trust and that it's endlessly stressful to be engaged in a relationship that requires continuous proof of safe footing.

Each day in a relationship has the quality of an Indiana Jones adventure. Each day will be a test of faith. If you require proof of permanent safety each day, both you and your partner will be quickly exhausted in the attempt and the fun will rapidly leave the adventure. This is especially true since partners can never convincingly prove that they won't leave, only that so far they haven't.

The alternative to distrust is to <u>choose</u> to trust both your partner and your future in the relationship. This isn't the same as believing that you know for certain that all will be well. Based on experience with and knowledge of your partner, you make an educated guess. It means that, even in the absence of certainty, you choose to proceed as if you were certain. Just like Indiana Jones, it's only by moving forward as if you were sure that the bridge was there that you can in fact find the bridge.

♥

Whether it's "don't ask" or "don't tell",
the marriage gets weaker and weaker.

♥

Don't wait 'til it's too late

*L*ike any living organism, a marriage can die from a lack of nurturance. For any relationship it is possible to get to a point of no return, where the strength and resilience of the relationship is so diminished that it cannot be revived.

Sid and Lori sat in the office, Lori on a chair by herself despite Sid's invitation to sit next to him on the couch. Lori looked relatively bored. Sid looked anxious.

When asked what brought them in, Sid answered immediately, while Lori sat quietly, looking detached. "It's our marriage. We need help saving it. We're desperate." Lori didn't look even a little desperate. She didn't even look interested.

"Lori?"

"Well, Sid's desperate. Frankly, I don't much care anymore."

"Why is that, Lori?"

"Look, for years I waited patiently for Sid to become the husband that I wanted. It never happened. I guess I got tired of waiting. I put my energy into other things – the kids, the house, my career. Now those are the things that matter to me. The marriage doesn't."

"So tell me, Lori, what have you tried in an effort to make this marriage work for you?"

"Try? I didn't try anything. I figured the best thing to do was wait patiently. No way I was going to become a nag or one of those women who complain all the time."

"Sid, when did you realize that your marriage was in serious trouble?"

"That's just it. I had no idea. I thought we were fine. I only just figured out that things were so bad when Lori suggested that perhaps a separation might be a good idea. I thought she was joking, but she had been looking in the paper for apartments for me. She showed me some places that she thought looked affordable. I thought we were fine and now I'm looking at affordable apartments!"

Sid's agitation was intense. Lori's detachment was cool and pervasive. Marital therapy in this case looked like it might be an attempt to resuscitate a body that was already cold.

As the therapist, what I most wanted at that moment was a time machine. I wanted a way to travel back in time to an earlier moment in this marriage. I wanted to revisit that choice point when Lori could have chosen to share with Sid her needs and disappointments instead of keeping it to herself. Of course, I also wanted to go back to a moment when Sid could have taken the initiative to ask Lori if there was anything that he could do to better meet her needs. In real time, when Lori could have spoken, she chose instead to keep silent in hopes of preserving her image as the easygoing partner. She thought it was unseemly and even dangerous to rock the boat. Sid chose to take her silence as a confirmation of their success, even though he never checked that that impression was justified. He figured, why rock the boat?

So if nobody rocked the boat, why is it sinking?

It can be really hard to tell your partner that you're unhappy, especially if you've been taught not to "complain". It can be just as hard to hear that your partner is unhappy, and so sometimes we avoid asking or we give covert messages that we don't want to hear. Both of these strategies preserve peace and comfort, at least in the short term. The problem is, they lay a foundation of not communicating. Whether it's "don't ask" or "don't tell", either way the result is that the fabric of the marriage gets weaker and weaker. The attempt to preserve peace in the short term creates either explosive eruptions or the cold quiet of disinterest in the long term.

Marriage is meant for the long term. That means committing yourself not to short term comfort but to long term success. And that means learning strategies that maximize communication and honesty. Marriage is not for wimps. It takes courage to give up familiar ways of avoiding trouble. It takes courage to share your most sensitive feelings and courage to hear when you need to do things differently. Ask yourself, do you want a moment of peace or a marriage that will last through the years? Go rock the boat. Do it now, before it's too late.

♥

Each action has a direct effect on the other
and a rebound effect on the self.

♥

A spiritual union

*T*hey met at a family reunion, but neither belonged to the family. She came with her best friend, who'd begged her to come along and be a buffer between her and her mom. He came with his racquetball buddy, who was hoping to persuade his little brother to go to their mutual business school instead of backpack around South America. They found each other around the grill, each hoping for the first properly incinerated hot dog. It was a match made in heaven.

They started dating and found their bond deepening. She began to long for each phone call, each chance to spend time together. He felt like the only days that counted were the ones spent with her. They felt like they only breathed properly when they were together.

Colors were brighter, music sweeter, the weather gentler. The world felt like a different place. It surprised exactly no one when they announced their wedding plans.

Even the wedding planning was loving, although it wasn't particularly elaborate. Each detail was considered for how it made the other partner feel. The wedding wasn't formal, but it felt sacred. They'd written their own vows, which affirmed their love and pledged eternity to one another. They looked deeply into each other's eyes as they exchanged rings. The kiss sent a shiver down everyone's spines, as if it vibrated through the years yet to come. Couples who'd been married for years took each other's hands and exchanged looks that reaffirmed their own vows. Everybody agreed afterward that it had been a uniquely spiritual event.

Their first year had as many ups and downs as anyone's. They were sentimental about every silly anniversary, like the two-month anniversary of their first big appliance purchase, or the one-month anniversary of the first time they had pizza as husband and wife. They quarreled over his persistent lateness and over her bathroom messiness. They had to deal with her migraines and his bad back. It was no more a perfect year than anybody else's.

People noticed that throughout the year and through all of its challenges they seemed to become closer and more committed to each other. Even when she was irritated with him, she seemed to be able to find her way toward him with kindness. Even when he was annoyed with her, he seemed to reach beyond it with gentleness toward her. It wasn't clear that they had fewer fights than other couples, but the fights seemed to end more quickly and with less wounding. They seemed to find their way back to each other as if with a compass.

There were some years that were easy and some that were hard. They weren't happy with each other every single minute; and sometimes they were angry or disappointed. But they seemed to be grounded in a kind of general rule – they tried to be aware always of each other's deepest feelings, of what would cause hurt or fear. Always the awareness of the other's pain or anxiety would serve as a beacon to lead them back to kindness and gentleness.

As is common during a 50th wedding anniversary party, someone asked the secret of their successful marriage. She smiled at her husband of 50 years and said, "I always believed that I nurtured <u>my</u> spirit when I tended to his."

He smiled warmly at her and said, "I always felt that our union was sacred. My spirit was injured anytime that I reached out with anger or harshness toward her, since I knew that <u>her</u> spirit would be hurt."

Each action was understood to have both a direct effect on the other and a rebound effect on the self. Kindness given was balm to the self. Gentleness extended was food for the soul of the giver. It turns out that doing unto others, especially a loved one, <u>is</u> doing unto oneself.

Conclusion

As with any journey, this one starts with the first step. With *How to Get and Give Love – Relationship Maps*, you should be able to feel that you are better prepared to meet the challenges along your path. You now have had a course in the process of joining with a partner to meet your own and your partner's needs. Whatever may present itself along your roadways, the key isn't necessarily to know the answer, but knowing how to work with a partner to find an answer that works for both of you.

How to Get and Give Love – Relationship Maps uses a three component model – *Listening, Understanding, and Responding* – to help you accomplish that goal. By implementing these three components, in the prescribed order, it should be possible for two committed people to achieve a mutually satisfactory objective.

I truly believe that most people are doing the best they know how to do in their relationships. A variety of things can interfere with that effort being successful. One of the most common is the interference of an old "map". We all bring our own histories into relationships, for better or for worse. Critical to the success of any relationship is the efforts of both parties to craft a new and evolved map that is well suited to the challenges of Here and Now.

As C. Swindall said, "We are all faced with a series of great opportunities brilliantly disguised as impossible situations."

I wish for you many great opportunities. Perhaps after reading this book, you'll find them to be less impossible-looking.

Made in the USA
Columbia, SC
09 September 2018